# Saved by Grace...

*Ephesians 2: 8*

# Judged According to Works

*Revelation 20: 12*

By

*Steven A. Carlson*

GUARDIAN
PUBLISHING, LLC

This edition published in November 2021 in association with

**Guardian Publishing, LLC**
**Holt, Michigan**

guardianpublishingllc.com

## Other Books Available from Guardian Publishing, LLC:

**Baptism and the Battle for Souls** – *Faith that Demands Obedience*
**Baptism and the Plan of Salvation** – *Restoring the New Testament Gospel*
**Pentecost** – *The Sanctioning of the Apostles*
**One Bible…And Yet, So Many Beliefs** – *Exploring the Doctrinal Chaos*
**Christian Principles: Raising the Bar** – *Engaging Lessons from the Sermon on the Mount*
**Born of Water and the Spirit** – *Entering the Kingdom*
**Good News for Everyone!** – *Life-Changing Encounters in the Gospel of John*
**Did Jesus Descend into Hell?** – *Biblical Insights into a Curious Proposition*

All Scripture quotations, unless otherwise noted, are taken from the Holy Bible: New American Standard Version (NASV), Copyright © 2002. Used by permission of the Zondervan Corporation, all rights reserved.

# In Memoriam

*As I was concluding the writing of this book, I experienced a sad occasion with the loss of my brother-in-law, Dewey Nash. Dewey was an outstanding Christian man and has undoubtedly joined with the saints in heaven. In that regard, I am happy for him. It must be an unimaginable improvement after the struggle with cancer that he faced in his physical body.*

*Dewey will be missed, not merely as a family member, but as an exceptional life-long mate to my sister and a very dear friend to everyone in the family. Sadly, we were separated by far too many miles in this life, but on those occasions when we were together, it was always a joy to see his broad smile, witness his strong work ethic, and embrace the wisdom that was evident in his every word. I am honored to submit this work to you in his memory.*

*Thank you for your life and friendship, Dewey.*
*You are sorely missed.*

# Table of Contents

| Title | Page |
|---|---|

# Preface

While this book, or at least the idea of this book, has been on my mind for quite some time, I have delayed starting it for a number of reasons. One reason for the delay is that I was concentrating on some other works that required serious commitment. Although, while this is true, perhaps the primary reason for my hesitation was recognition of the fact that this is a most challenging topic.

A challenge has never dissuaded me in the past, as I have written on subjects that many would consider difficult, but this one seems different. The subject itself is not particularly complex, but it is multi-faceted and highly misunderstood. Much of the reason for this misunderstanding is that biblical instruction about the relationship between grace, faith, and works has become clouded over time.

Scripture is unambiguous when it comes to a person's opportunity for redemption. By God's grace, eternal salvation has been made available to mankind. Absent that grace, no one would or could be saved given the manner in which sin has permeated every facet of human life. Similarly, faith is necessary for an individual to realize saved status. Most believers agree on these tenets of Christianity.

God's Word is also clear that no one can earn his/her way to heaven by performing good works since works cannot wash away sins. This cleansing is only available through the shed blood of Jesus Christ. Even

1

the blood sacrifices of the Old Testament were insufficient when it came to cleansing humankind of sin.

If the opportunity for redemption is made available by God's grace and salvation is attained through faith as opposed to good deeds (Ephesians 2: 8-9), why would the Apostle John declare that people will be judged according to their works (Revelation 20: 12)? Is this a biblical contradiction? Has the apostle made a grievous error?

The following pages offer a biblical discussion of the relationship between grace, faith, and works, including a look into exactly what John meant when he stated that judgment will be *according to works*. Additionally, attention will be given to the difference between obedience to God's commands and performing good works – an important biblical distinction with eternal consequences.

# Chapter One
# The Five Solae

## The Printing Press

The year was AD 1440 and the man's name was Johannes Gutenberg (1398-1468) – a German goldsmith by trade. On January 1st of that year, Gutenberg introduced the initial design of the first printing press to the world. Other methods of mechanical, moveable type printing using wood block lettering had been introduced in places like China as early as the ninth century, but this was the first time a design had been developed with mass production in view. The press was designed based on the mechanical principles of the traditional screw press, which was a precursor to the modern drill press.

Within a decade, a workable model was constructed and ready for use. It should surprise no one that the first published document was the Bible (in Latin), which was completed and introduced to the public commercially in 1454, but the cost was prohibitive. At the time, a copy of the Bible would cost three years' wages for the average man.

Johannes Gutenberg died in 1468. Unfortunately, due to lawsuits and exorbitant costs, Gutenberg never really profited from his efforts. Still, he is remembered today as a man who was largely responsible for changing the direction of the world of mankind educationally, philosophically, politically, and religiously.

As production costs improved and commercial pricing fell in line, the Bible became more available to the common man. There is a strong argument that the availability of Scripture to the general public helped usher in what is now known as the Reformation Movement of the sixteenth century.

## The Reformation Movement

Over the course of time, the Roman Catholic Church (RCC) developed practices and assorted rituals that seemed to challenge the biblical teaching that salvation is a matter of faith. These teachings were accepted by the common man primarily because he had no accessibility to godly instruction against which church teachings could be measured. Consequently, what the church taught was recognized by most people as biblical truth.

By the beginning of the sixteenth century, the Bible was readily available to the masses. It was during this time that a priest by the name of Martin Luther (1483-1546) began to publicly question some of the teachings of the RCC, which he believed depicted forgiveness/salvation as a matter of works and/or payments. The availability of Scripture to the general public allowed him to draw support from that public.

In late 1517, Martin Luther posted a document on the door of the castle church in Wittenberg titled *Ninety-Five Theses*. In it he challenged, and even condemned, the selling of indulgences along with many other RCC practices that he deemed antithetical to the biblical theme of salvation as a matter of faith. He focused on the need for honest repentance, insisting that these practices were misleading and, consequently, harming the church. According to Luther, neither those who were paying for indulgences nor those who were selling them were being sincere about grace and repentance. The selling of indulgences had deteriorated into a strictly financial transaction. The posting of *Ninety-Five Theses* is recognized by many as the starting point of what has come to be known as the Reformation Movement.

Luther's document was cumbersome, consisting of ninety-five charges against the church, so committing them to memory was difficult. Later, in an effort to simplify the theme of *Ninety-Five Theses*, five Latin phrases were adopted that seemed to embody the core principles of the Reformation Movement. Known as the *Five Solae*, in simple terms they challenged many of the teachings that the RCC had developed over more than a millennium. The phrases and their meanings were as follows:

| **Phrase** | **Meaning** |
|---|---|
| • Sola Scriptura | Scripture alone |
| • Soli Deo Gloria | The Glory of God alone |
| • Solus Christus | Christ alone |
| • Sola Gratia | Grace alone |
| • Sola Fide | Faith alone |

While many like to attribute authorship of the *Five Solae* to Martin Luther, there is no evidence that he wrote them. In fact, it is unlikely that they were written during Luther's lifetime. While the message they contain clearly derived from the Protestant Reformation arguments, the fact that they are not cited directly in known sixteenth century literature suggests a much later date. It is likely that an individual or group developed these terms at some point in time after men like Luther, who had laid the groundwork in the early sixteenth century, had departed this life.

## Sola

The intent behind the final three solae is that salvation is found *in Christ alone*, made available *by grace alone*, and received *through faith alone*. That is to say, Christ is the *source* of salvation, grace is the *offering* of salvation, and faith is the *condition* of salvation. This language served a specific purpose where the Reformers were concerned. They hoped to counteract the practices of the RCC by focusing attention on scriptural instruction concerning redemption. The idea was that *Christ, grace,* and *faith* accurately portrayed biblical instruction with respect to salvation, and the current practices of the church (e.g., the requirement of penance for forgiveness and the sale of indulgences), which were not scripturally based, should not be added to them.

The introduction of the *Five Solae* heavily influenced Christendom in that they led to a new view of Scripture. This would result in philosophies that men like Luther probably never envisioned. The problem was the specific wording that was employed by the Reformers to express their ideas. After some time, rather than focusing on Christ, grace, and faith, which was the intent, many people began to focus on the word *sola,* meaning *alone.* This word eventually came to eclipse the biblical principles that the *Five Solae* sought to advance.

> After some time, rather than focusing on Christ, grace, and faith...many people began to focus on the word *sola,* meaning *alone.*

Paul wrote, "[8]For by grace you have been saved through faith...[9]not as a result of works" (Ephesians 2: 8-9), and his words are absolutely

6

true. Yet, the focus on *sola* rather than the biblical pillars of grace and faith caused many to begin to criticize, and eventually decry, any teaching of a relationship between faith and works. Consequently, faith became redefined as *belief only*, but this was not Paul's intent.

While Paul declared unambiguously that salvation is a matter of faith, salvific faith is not defined in the Ephesians text. When the full biblical portrait of faith is discovered, it becomes clear that the faith of Scripture is not, as many like to claim, a matter of simply believing in Jesus.

## The Book of James

Martin Luther strongly opposed church teachings that, in his view, smacked of salvation by works. In fact, he was so steadfast in his beliefs that, although he never actually insisted that the book of James should be removed from the Bible, he openly rejected certain teachings in the epistle where the connection between works and faith is emphasized. According to Luther, James's words flew in the face of the gospel message as he understood it. He wrote:

> Therefore St James' epistle is really an epistle of straw, compared to these others, for it has nothing of the nature of the Gospel about it.[1]

Despite Luther's struggle, James never taught that a person could be saved by works. Anyone who believes that James taught salvation by works has misread his words. By all accounts, Luther was a forthright man who should have understood what James was saying, but the point of the letter seems to have eluded him. Perhaps the reason he took issue

---

[1] Did Martin Luther Really Want James Taken Out of... | Zondervan Academic, accessed Jun 10, 2021.

with James is that he was heavily engrossed in his fight against the practices and teachings of the RCC that seemed to depict salvation as a matter of works. Consequently, the idea of a biblical connection between faith and works was anathema to him.

For those who insist that James contradicts Paul's teaching by linking faith and works, nothing could be further from the truth. In fact, the book of James arguably provides one of the most important lessons of Scripture and it is a lesson that complements Paul's teaching about salvation through faith. For those who seek to understand salvation through faith, James offers instruction that is critical to the life of the believer. That instruction will be discussed in depth in Chapter Three where teaching concerning the character of biblical faith is discussed in greater depth.

# Chapter Two
# Understanding Grace

## Grace

The concept of biblical grace is often misunderstood, partly due to a lack of appreciation for the concept of grace generally. To many who proclaim belief in Jesus, grace is simply that magical, mystical part of the gospel message that precedes faith in Paul's words to the church in Ephesus. When Paul proclaimed to the Ephesians "For by grace you have been saved..." (Ephesians 2: 8), he was identifying grace, not as a declaration of redemption, but as God's *offer* of salvation to mankind.

In order to understand grace, it is necessary to understand who has standing to offer grace, both biblically and generally. After all, not everyone is in a position to extend an offer of grace. For instance, a debtor cannot offer grace to the one to whom a debt is owed. Conversely, the person owed *is* in a position to offer grace to his/her debtor.

The concept of grace cannot be fully understood without a basic grasp of what might be considered *the natural rule of debt*. In order to appreciate grace, it is necessary to recognize that every debt is paid. Every debt that has ever been owed, is currently owed, or will be owed in the future, is eventually paid. Even liberal bankruptcy laws cannot circumvent this natural reality concerning satisfaction of debt.

Some may look at the idea of *the natural rule of debt* and wonder how this can be. Others may even begin citing debts that they believe were never satisfied – perhaps even their own debts – but this misses the point. When it comes

> ...the question is not: *Will a debt be paid?* The relevant question is: *Who will pay the debt?*

to payment of debt – any debt – the question is not: *Will a debt be paid?* The relevant question is: *Who will pay the debt?* The answer to this question explains the truth behind *the natural rule of debt.*

It stands to reason that, at least most of the time, it is the debtor who pays what is owed. It seems this must be true, otherwise it is unlikely that anyone, whether an individual or a business, would ever willingly make a loan to another person or business. If most people failed to pay their debts, the risk of making a loan would be far too high.

There are other times when a debt is not actually paid by the debtor. Sometimes people simply fail to pay while others file bankruptcy or seek other means to escape the responsibility of payment. When this happens, the debt is still paid, but it is paid by the one to whom the debt is owed. Rather than being paid from the account of the debtor, there is a shortage in the lender's account that is *equal to* the debt that remained unpaid by the debtor. In such a case, the debtor has effectively forced the lender to pay the amount of the debt from the lender's own coffers.

Grace comes into play when a lender *offers to forgive* a debt that is owed. In such a case, once again, the debt is paid, but it is willingly and gracefully satisfied by the lender. Jesus spoke of such a situation in his parable of the unmerciful servant (Matthew 18: 23-34). In that case, a servant who could not pay his debt to the king begged for mercy.

Generously, the king offered to forgive the debt. In other words, the king was willing to satisfy the debt by paying it himself.

While the discussion thus far has focused on lending, and even more specifically on monetary lending, not every debt is financial in character. Some debts are far more personal and there are certain debts that a debtor may never be able to repay. As an example, if a person saves someone's life, especially through the sacrifice of his own life (which can easily happen on the battlefield during war), it is a debt the debtor will never really repay. Yet, it is a debt that has already been satisfied with the life that was freely given. Nothing more is expected from the one whose life was saved. Forgiveness of such a debt is inherent in the act of sacrifice.

## Act of Grace

Grace *always* involves both volition and action on the part of the one who offers grace to another. It involves volition in that grace can never be taken by force. It requires that a decision be made by the grantor since grace can only be offered willingly. Neither can grace be earned since this is simply another manner of *paying* the debt that is owed.

In the case of the king who offered grace to his servant (above), it involved the king's *decision* to forgive the servant's debt and the subtle and silent act of *paying* from his own coffers what the servant owed. Where one person gives his/her life to save another, the decision, which may be made in the blink of an eye, and the act involved are rather obvious.

11

## Heavenly Grace

The (spiritual) grace that God has offered humankind differs slightly from common grace that is offered between men. It is an elevated grace since it involves salvation/eternal life. Yet, grace does not equal salvation, or every person would be saved since God has offered grace to everyone on earth (cf. 2 Peter 3: 9).

When Paul wrote "For by grace you have been saved..." (Ephesians 2: 8), it was not a proclamation concerning *how* people are saved. Grace is not the source of salvation, but the vehicle God has made available for humankind to be reconciled to him. To put this in layman's terms, suppose a man wanted to travel abroad from the United States...perhaps to Europe. When asked how he got to Europe, he might rightfully answer, "I came by plane." Yet, the plane was not the reason that individual arrived in Europe. The plane was simply his means of transportation...a means available to any and all who chose to avail themselves of the opportunity.

The reason the man was in Europe – what got him there – was his decision to buy a ticket and board the plane. The choices he made led to his arrival in a foreign country. Had he not acted to procure his seat, the plane would still have arrived in Europe, but the man would not. It is in this same sense that Paul used the terminology "...by grace you have been saved..." Grace is not the reason a person is saved, but the means (or vehicle) by which a person's journey to salvation is made available. Max Lucado made this point, writing: "Though grace is available to all, it is accepted by few."[2]

---

[2] Lucado, Max, *In the Grip of Grace: Your Father Always Caught You. He Still Does*, Thomas Nelson, Nashville, Mexico City, Rio De Janeiro, 2014, p. 98.

## The Source of Salvation

When Adam and Eve sinned, death followed. Death was and is a consequence of sin. God made this clear to Adam and Eve, warning them, "…from the tree of the knowledge of good and evil you shall not eat, for on the day that you eat from it you will certainly die." (Genesis 2: 17). With that statement, God declared that payment for sin was death (cf. Romans 6: 23).

It is natural for men to view God's warning to Adam and Eve in terms of physical death. After all, he did say "…on the day that you eat…you will certainly die." Yet, the couple did not die physically on that day. This can only mean that God was not visualizing immediate physical death when he spoke, although ultimate physical death was seemingly masked within his words. This must be true since, shortly thereafter, God refused them access to the tree of life so they could no longer eat its fruit and live forever on earth (Genesis 3: 22-24).

Since Adam and Eve did not die physically on the day they sinned, God must have had something else – another kind of death – in view. Scripture reveals that the initial death Adam and Eve experienced was spiritual death (cf. Ephesians 2: 1-3; James 1: 15). The purity of their connection with God – the source of undefiled spiritual life for humankind – was severed. They were separated from God spiritually and would not, from that day forward, know the kind of relationship with him that they had experienced prior to their sin.

The example of Adam and Eve demonstrates that there are two aspects to mankind's debt to God. The first is a physical debt. When someone sins, absent special provision from God, that person's physical life is required as a matter of payment. There is also a spiritual aspect to

13

this debt. That is seen in one's separation from God (spiritual death). Physical death does not restore that relationship; it only settles the physical debt.

With the exception of those who remain alive at the Parousia (Second Coming) and certain people for whom God has made special provision (example, Enoch), every person will experience physical death in payment for his/her own sins (cf. Romans 6: 23). This is the consequence of sin proclaimed by God. Reconciliation to God, the spiritual part of the debt, also required death, but not just any death. The only death that would suffice was the death of one who owed God no payment for his own sins.

The trouble with someone offering up a sinless life to God is that no human being in a position to sacrifice himself for others can claim a sinless existence (cf. Romans 3: 23). Consequently, the only solution was for God to become man, live a sinless life, and then offer that life on behalf of humankind. Jesus' death on the cross constitutes the decisive *act of grace* that was necessary to satisfy this spiritual debt. Like the king in the parable, God chose to pay from his own coffers the debt that was owed. This is what Jesus did and this is why he is portrayed in Scripture as the source of eternal life (cf. John 14: 6; Acts 4: 12).

# Chapter Three
# Defining Faith

## Faith

The title *Defining Faith* that heads this chapter can be read and appreciated from two perspectives. That is because the word *defining*, which is a participle, can be employed as either a verb or an adjective. On one hand, it can be used as a verb to define faith. That is part of the goal here. In this chapter, the objective is to understand the concept of faith from a biblical perspective.

On the other hand, a participle can serve as an adjective. In that case, this word might be seen as addressing the character, or substance, of faith. A person may claim to have faith in another person, but *defining faith* characterizes the depth of that faith. It portrays the level of trust in the relationship. It is a *defining faith*. The deepest trust, or faith, naturally translates into actions that reflect the deep-seated character of that trust such as a willingness to place in the care of another person those things that are personally most precious (life, family, etc.).

## Faith Defined

Paul reminded the Ephesians that they had been saved "...by grace...through faith" (Ephesians 2: 8), and a truer statement was never made. Although, it is generally unwise to pluck a single passage from God's Word and deem it to be the sole guiding testimony on any topic. It is necessary to consider this teaching and how it harmonizes with the larger biblical landscape and the breadth of instruction that is available concerning the relationship between grace, faith, and salvation.

Many seem to view the concept of faith purely in terms of what a person thinks or believes. To them, biblical faith is simply recognition and acceptance of the truth that Jesus, as God, came to earth and sacrificed himself for the sins of the world. This view of faith fails to take into account the fullness of Scripture. Consider the following verses where belief is portrayed as falling short of faith.

> Nevertheless many, even of the rulers, believed in Him, but because of the Pharisees they were not confessing *Him*, so that they would not be excommunicated from the synagogue. (John 12: 42)

> You believe that God is one. You do well; the demons also believe, and shudder. (James 2: 19)

God's Word employs some form of the term *faith* (Gr. *pistis*) dozens of times (e.g., faith, faithful, faithfulness). When it comes to understanding biblical teaching about faith, it is clear that the faith of Scripture is seen in faithfulness, or faithful *action*. One biblical illustration is provided in a woman by the name of Lydia. When Lydia responded to the gospel message, she noted that her submission to baptism was a matter of faithful obedience (Acts 16: 15).

Where the Apostle Paul is concerned, he wrote often of faith as a matter of faithful action. This is seen in his consistent recognition of the faithfulness of the believers to whom he wrote his letters as well as his consistent call for them to remain faithful.

> But the fruit of the Spirit is love, joy, peace, patience, kindness, goodness, **faithfulness**. (Galatians 5: 22) emphasis added

> Paul, an apostle of Christ Jesus by the will of God, To the saints who are at Ephesus and *are* **faithful** in Christ Jesus (Ephesians 1: 1) emphasis added

To the saints and **faithful** brothers *and sisters* in Christ *who are* at Colossae: Grace to you and peace from God our Father. (Colossians 1: 2) emphasis added

Women *must* likewise *be* dignified, not malicious gossips, but temperate, **faithful** in all things. (1 Timothy 3: 11) emphasis added

The things which you have heard from me in the presence of many witnesses, entrust these to **faithful** people who will be able to teach others also. (2 Timothy 2: 2) emphasis added

Even with Paul's use of the terms faithful and faithfulness, he never really defined faith for his readers. That is not to say that Scripture leaves faith undefined. It is well-defined both in the book of Hebrews and in the book of James. In that sense, those works complement the Apostle Paul's teaching by offering clearer insight into what constitutes the faith of the Bible.

Some say Paul penned the book of Hebrews, but confidence in Paul's authorship is not strong. Others attribute the work to Barnabas, Paul's traveling companion. Still others believe the letter was written by either Apollos or another early disciple who wrote under the guidance of the apostles. Nonetheless, the author of this letter has provided what many consider to be the most concise (Webster-like) definition of faith Scripture has to offer, stating:

Now faith is *the* certainty of *things* hoped for, a proof of things not seen. (Hebrews 11: 1)

Two key words stick out in this verse, each of which is intended to provide insight into what constitutes biblical faith. The first is the word *certainty* (Gr. *hypostasis*). It is rendered variously in other English translations. For example, the KJV uses the word *substance* while the NIV translates this term with the English word *confidence*. In the RSV and NRSV, it is rendered *assurance*.

17

Although this verse offers the kind of description one might expect to find in a dictionary, the wording is not that easy to follow, which is why it has been translated into English with such diversity, using words that hold different meanings for different people. To many people, the term *substance* points, not to belief, but to truth. This is one of the better translations for the Greek term since it speaks to the integrity of that which is believed. If something is substantive, it is considered reliable. On the other hand, *certainty* and *confidence* speak to personal internal belief while *assurance* generally comes from an outside source. Other translations use such words as *reality* (HSBC) and *being sure* (NLT). Adam Clark (1762-1832) has offered one of the better explanations of the writer's use of this word:

> The word υποστασις, which we translate *substance*, signifies *subsistence*, that which becomes a *foundation* for another thing to stand on.[3]

The second term that jumps off the page is the word *proof* (Gr. *elenchus*). Like *hypostasis,* this word has been translated into English using assorted terminology in this setting. The KJV employs the term *evidence* while the NIV has translated it as *assurance* (the very word the RSV and NRSV apply to *hypostasis*). The word *conviction* appears in the RSV and NRSV as the English translation for the Greek *elenchus*. Again, these words hold different meanings among English-speaking people, so the verse, as written, offers a rather blurred definition for faith. The reason for this is that this verse is not intended to provide a conventional definition of faith. Instead, the purpose of this verse is to introduce the balance of the chapter where the ideas presented

---

[3] Clark, Adam, *Clark's Commentaries, Volume VI, Romans – Revelation*, Abingdon-Cokesbury Press, New York/Nashville, p. 762.

in the first verse are exemplified. In other words, the entire chapter (Hebrews 11) serves as a definition, or description, of biblical faith.

The translation of *conviction* for the Greek *elenchus* seems most reasonable since it suggests more than thoughtful reflection. The idea behind this verse is that faith eclipses merely accepting that something is true. Clark wrote concerning the use of *elenchus* in this verse:

> And ελεγχος signifies such a *conviction* as is produced in the mind by the *demonstration* of a *problem*, after which demonstration no doubt can remain, because we see from it that the thing *is*; that it *cannot but be*; and that it cannot be *otherwise* than as it is, and is proved to be.[4]

What the biblical writer seemed to be teaching with his combination of *hypostasis* and *elenchus* is that faith should be understood as one's *reliance upon* what is hoped for and yet unseen. Faith goes beyond someone recognizing the truth in that the person's decisions are dependent on his/her conviction concerning that truth. This is the faith that is demonstrated in the balance of the chapter where belief and deeds go hand in hand as individuals' actions were grounded fully in their trust in God.

## Faith In Action

It is important to understand the words of Scripture. In order to do this, it is equally important to give honest consideration to the context of the written word, but there is a factor that can be distracting, making it a bit difficult to recognize context. In the late sixteenth century, with the release of the Geneva Bible, chapters and verses were introduced into the text.

---

[4] Ibid

When God's Word was penned, the authors wrote letters, or books, that could be read and appreciated for the richness of their message. The artificial addition of chapters and verses, which admittedly make it much easier to locate specific passages, has resulted in a misconception for many readers. It is often thought that one can begin reading at the beginning of a particular chapter without missing the bigger picture, but this is not always the case.

The final verses in the tenth chapter that lead up to the definition of faith given in the eleventh chapter of Hebrews are as relevant as the verses that follow. They equally address the idea of faith that is presented in the text.

> [36] For you have need of endurance, so that when you have done the will of God, you may receive what was promised.
> [37] FOR YET IN A VERY LITTLE WHILE,
> HE WHO IS COMING WILL COME, AND WILL NOT DELAY.
> [38] BUT MY RIGHTEOUS ONE WILL LIVE BY FAITH;
> AND IF HE SHRINKS BACK, MY SOUL HAS NO PLEASURE IN HIM.
> [39] But we are not among those who shrink back to destruction, but of those who have faith for the safekeeping of the soul. (Hebrews 10: 36-39)

These verses give a larger perspective on the idea of personal faith in God. Faith is presented in terms of doing God's will (v. 36) and living by faith (v. 38). It is these thoughts that introduce the foundational perspective on faith that is offered in the eleventh chapter. In other words, faith in God is not merely a matter of the mind – it is a matter of life. It is a way of life that involves the decisions and actions of those who wish to be of the faith.

The initial *definition* of faith (Hebrews 11: 1) is followed with what the author evidently considered further clarification of that definition.

He began by offering a portrait of the unseen upon which people rely, stating:

> [2] For by it (faith) the people of old gained approval. [3] By faith we understand that the world has been created by the word of God so that what is seen has not been made out of things that are visible. (Hebrews 11: 2-3)

The faith of Scripture, according to the writer, is built on the foundational principle that God is all powerful, and that he created all that exists within the world of humanity. This is in keeping with his definition of faith where it is presented as that upon which one relies in making life choices.

What follows in the eleventh chapter of Hebrews is a look at many examples of historical individuals whose lives embodied that faith. What the writer has provided in the ensuing verses is insight into the character of biblical faith. When it comes to the examples provided, it becomes clear that faith to them meant much more than mere belief.

It should go without saying that the New Testament, from which modern believers glean truth about Jesus, was unavailable when the book of Hebrews was written since this book is part of that New Testament. Consequently, when the author sought to provide his readers with demonstrations of faith, he turned to the Old Testament faithful as examples of faith in action.

The conviction of the Old Testament faithful concerning God was what led to the decisions they made. That is to say, they were so confident in their view of God that they made their most significant life decisions relying on the substantive character of their beliefs. They were willing, based on their conviction, to put everything on the line, including their lives and the lives of their loved ones. From this point forward in Hebrews 11, faith is depicted in the actions of those who believed in and were faithful to God.

The first of the faithful mentioned in this chapter is Abel, the second son of Adam and Eve. According to the author, it was his conviction that led him to offer an acceptable offering to God while his elder brother, Cain, who lacked conviction, gave an unacceptable offering (Hebrews 11: 4). Abel's faith was reflected in his faithful giving. While many may consider an offering seemingly inconsequential when compared to life and death decisions, note that Abel's life was taken due to his faithfulness in giving (Genesis 4: 8).

This reminder of Abel's faith is followed by a look into the life of Enoch, who was Noah's grandfather. While his specific actions are not detailed, his belief in God was revealed in his life decisions. Due to his faithfulness, Enoch was taken from this earth without experiencing death. According to the author, "…he was attested to have been pleasing to God" (Hebrews 11: 5), not just for what he *believed*, but for what he *did* based on the strength of his conviction.

It is also written that, based on his faith in God, Noah built a massive ark (Hebrews 11: 7). Some have suggested that he may have spent decades preparing the ark (Genesis 6-7), although the precise amount of time it took is unknown. This was truly an act of faith since there is biblical evidence that, prior to the flood, it had never rained on the earth (Genesis 2: 5-6). Even if God had previously sent rain, the earth had never been destroyed by a flood, so building an ark required true conviction on Noah's part.

The chapter continues, reviewing the lives of many in the Old Testament who had made life decisions, living in accordance with their conviction. This includes Abraham and Sara (Hebrews 11: 8-12). In fact, Abraham's faith was so powerful that he was even willing to offer the life of his son simply because God asked it of

> **Abraham's faith was so powerful that he was even willing to offer the life of his son.**

him (Hebrews 11: 17-19). There is no doubt that, had an angel failed to stop him (Genesis 22: 11-12), Abraham would have sacrificed Isaac.

Several other Old Testament characters are mentioned whose actions were grounded in faith including Isaac, Moses, Rahab, Gideon, and many others. The author also notes that some had been flogged, tortured, and imprisoned for their conviction (vv. 35-36). Others were stoned to death, sawn in two, or killed by the sword for their faith (v. 37).

The words in the balance of Hebrews 11 are intended to complement Paul's words concerning faith. While Paul taught that people are saved through faith, Hebrews provides insight into what faith looks like. This chapter in Hebrews goes far in offering support for James's teaching concerning the connection between faith and works that is discussed in detail in Chapter Four.

# Chapter Four
# James on Faith and Works

## The Faith/Works Connection

In keeping with Paul's teaching concerning salvation, Martin Luther preached that attaining eternal life was a matter of faith. For centuries, the practices of the RCC leaned strongly in favor of the doctrine that redemption involved a combination of works/payments, and Luther, who was a priest in the church, sought to overcome what he saw as misrepresentation of the gospel message. This is why he struggled so heavily with the canonization of the book of James, as noted earlier (see Chapter 1). His objection was grounded in the inescapable connection between faith and works on display in James's words.

Following in Luther's footsteps, modern teachers have often sought to minimalize James's teaching concerning salvation and works. Yet, the claim that James taught salvation by works represents a mischaracterization, or at least a misunderstanding, of his words. James did not teach that salvation could be earned, but he did establish a clear distinction between faith and the absence of faith. In that vein, he wrote the following.

[22] But prove yourselves doers of the word, and not just hearers who deceive themselves. [23] For if anyone is a hearer of the word and not a doer, he is like a man who looks at his natural face in a mirror; [24] for *once* he has looked at himself and gone away, he has immediately forgotten what kind of person he was. [25] But one who has looked intently at the perfect law, the *law* of freedom, and has continued *in it*, not having become a forgetful hearer but an active doer, this person will be blessed in what he does. (James 1: 22-25)

24

These words from James were not meant to be comforting to his readers. Rather than comforting them, he was challenging them, insisting that being a *doer* of the word is the very definition of faith. In modern times, where faith is narrowly defined as belief in God/Jesus, many have essentially disregarded James's instructions.

## Pseudo Faith

Not only did James fail to retreat from his position on the faith/works connection; he doubled down in the second chapter of his book where he offered the following instructions.

> [14] What use is it, my brothers *and sisters*, if someone says he has faith, but he has no works? Can that faith save him? [15] If a brother or sister is without clothing and in need of daily food, [16] and one of you says to them, "Go in peace, be warmed and be filled," yet you do not give them what is necessary for *their* body, what use is that? [17] In the same way, faith also, if it has no works, is dead, *being* by itself. [18] But someone may *well* say, "You have faith and I have works; show me your faith without the works, and I will show you my faith by my works." [19] You believe that God is one. You do well; the demons also believe, and shudder. [20] But are you willing to acknowledge, you foolish person, that faith without works is useless? (James 2: 14-20)

Many seem to bristle when reading this passage, insisting that it undercuts the biblical teaching of salvation as a matter of faith. That is because they have read the text through a tinted lens where faith and works must be divorced from one another. This has resulted in the teaching that, where salvation is concerned, any relationship between faith and works is not only unbiblical, but ungodly. The goal here is to overcome this misconception.

Approaching James's words as though he was attempting to command specific actions from his readers as a matter of salvation misses the point of the lesson. The fact of the matter is that, whether Christian or non-Christian, every person lives life in accordance with his/her beliefs. Those lives consist of decisions and actions (works). The Apostle Peter also recognized the significance of a person's actions, stating:

> If you address as Father the One who impartially judges according to each one's work, conduct yourselves in fear during the time of your stay *on earth* (1 Peter 1: 17)

In James 1: 22-25 (cited in the previous section), James envisioned a person who looked into God's Word and walked away leaving biblical instructions and godly principles behind him. He continued to live life in a manner that failed to reflect what he had learned from Scripture. He heard (or read) what God had to say, but it had no impact on his life. That man may have been a *hearer* of the Word, but he was certainly not a *doer*. It is difficult to argue that this man had developed a saving relationship with God.

Where James 2: 14-20 is concerned, the lesson was intended to hit closer to home for his immediate audience. While it might be argued that the person in the first passage (James 1: 22-25) may have walked away from biblical teachings without accepting Jesus, in the next passage, the words were aimed directly at the believers. James was addressing those who sought to compartmentalize their lives, separating the idea of faith from their actions. James would have no part of this.

Critical of the suggestion that faith can exist without works, James asked his readers, "What use is it, my brothers *and sisters*, if someone says he has faith, but he has no works? Can that faith save him?" (v. 14). The rhetorical nature of the question implies that the faith of such a person is not the faith described in the gospel message. This implication is further supported in the ensuing verses where examples of faith-driven works are provided. James wanted the believers to understand that inactive faith was inadequate where salvation was concerned.

The rhetorical question in verse fourteen is followed with a complementary query in the following verse, where James asked, "[15] If a brother or sister is without clothing and in need of daily food, [16] and one of you says to them, "Go in peace, be warmed and be filled," yet you do not give them what is necessary for *their* body, what use is that?" (vv. 15-16). His point with each of these questions was the same. Just as the hollow words of comfort in verse sixteen were meaningless, so faith without works lacks substance.

The example offered in the text, where James wrote of feeding and clothing someone in need, has served as a distraction for some and caused them to miss the heart of the lesson. His point was not about the importance of feeding and clothing those in need. It was not even about doing a good deed, *per se*. James wanted his audience to recognize that a person of faith will not live out their Christian walk sitting on the sidelines. They will participate in the work of the kingdom as a matter of godly worship (cf. Colossians 3: 17; Hebrews 12: 28).

## The Abraham Connection

James continued his thoughts on faith and works. Holding nothing back, he turned to name-dropping, reminding his readers of the man Abraham, whose life was an example for all to follow.

[21] Was our father Abraham not justified by works when he offered up his son Isaac on the altar? [22] You see that faith was working with his works, and as a result of the works, faith was perfected; [23] and the Scripture was fulfilled which says, "AND ABRAHAM BELIEVED GOD, AND IT WAS CREDITED TO HIM AS RIGHTEOUSNESS," and he was called a friend of God. [24] You see that a person is justified by works and not by faith alone. (James 2: 21-24)

With his final thought in this text (v. 24), James answered candidly the rhetorical question asked earlier (v. 14), perhaps out of concern that someone may have missed the point. This comment bothered Luther and it has continued to trouble many in the evangelical community, since it appears to contradict the teaching that salvation is a matter of *faith only*.

Much of the misunderstanding of James's teaching derives from a misapplication of the word *works* (Gr. *erga*) that appears in the text. When James wrote of the man who was "…a hearer of the word and not a doer" (James 1: 23), he understood that everyone, whether a believer or an unbeliever, continues to live his/her life on earth in human form and that life consist of decisions and actions. The believer whose decisions and actions reflect what has been learned from God's Word and honor God is the *doer* of whom James wrote.

The same holds true in James's comments concerning faith and works (James 2: 14-20). The example of an individual who failed to provide food and clothing for the person in need (vv. 15-16) was not intended as a *command* for the believers to seek out the poor and offer provision as a matter of redemption. Rather, James was distinguishing between the quasi faith of the person who offers only lip service in his walk with God and the response of the godly individual who is justified by faith.

The writer of the book of Hebrews offered depictions of faith by recalling actions of the Old Testament faithful and James declared "…as a result of works, faith was perfected" (James 2: 22). In this setting, the word translated *perfected* is *eteleiōthē* (from the Greek *teleion)*, which means *complete* (cf. Matthew 19: 21; Colossians 1: 28). In this verse, this is the translation found in assorted English versions of Scripture including some of the more recognized translations (e.g., ESV, NIV, NRSV, and RSV). This can only mean that, in James's view, Abraham's faith was perfected, or made complete, through his actions and, conversely, that faith absent works denotes incomplete faith.

> You see that faith was active along with his works, and faith was completed by his works. (James 2: 22, ESV)
>
> You see that his faith and his actions were working together, and his faith was made complete by what he did. (James 2: 22, NIV)
>
> You see that faith was active along with his works, and faith was brought to completion by the works. (James 2: 22, NRSV)
>
> You see that faith was active along with his works, and faith was completed by works. (James 2: 22, RSV)

## James vs Paul

What could James possibly have meant when, providing Abraham as an example, he stated that "…a person is justified by works, and not by faith alone" (v. 24)? Was he undermining Paul's teaching of salvation as a matter of faith? Was he not contradicting his own recognition that "ABRAHAM BELIEVED GOD, AND IT WAS CREDITED TO HIM AS RIGHTEOUSNESS" (V. 23)?

James was not contradicting Paul. In fact, his citation concerning Abraham's righteousness, which is from Genesis 15: 6, is the same text Paul cited in his letter to the Romans as he wrote concerning the relationship between faith and works.

> [1] What then shall we say that Abraham, our forefather according to the flesh, has found? [2] For if Abraham was justified by works, he has something to boast about; but not before God. [3] For what does the Scripture say? "ABRAHAM BELIEVED GOD, AND IT WAS CREDITED TO HIM AS RIGHTEOUSNESS." [4] Now to the one who works, the wages are not credited as a favor, but as what is due. [5] But to the one who does not work, but believes in Him who justifies the ungodly, his faith is credited as righteousness (Romans 4: 1-5)

How could two men of God, each of whose writings were chosen to be included in canonized Scripture, arrive at what appear to be diametrically opposing conclusions concerning the same Old Testament text? Paul stated unequivocally, citing Abraham as his example, that justification was not a result of works while James, using the same biblical example, wrote unapologetically that "…a person is justified by works, and not by faith alone" (v. 24). On the surface, it does not seem possible to find harmony between these two statements. Nonetheless, that harmony does exist.

> **How could two men of God…arrive at what appear to be diametrically opposing conclusions concerning the same Old Testament text?**

Through much of his ministry, Paul fought the teaching from many of the Jewish believers that Gentiles must first convert to Judaism if they wished to be followers of Christ. The difference between Paul's use of the word *works* (erga) and James's perspective is that Paul was challenging an attempt by the Jewish believers to force Gentile Christians in Rome to submit to the Mosaic Law and the rituals of the Abrahamic covenant. The issue of greatest concern appears to have been circumcision (Romans 4: 9-12). The *works* mentioned in this passage pointed directly and specifically to circumcision and the Mosaic Law.

Paul wanted the Jewish believers to recognize that justification through faith was nothing new. Even Abraham, the father of the Jewish nation, was justified by faith apart from the Law. When Paul wrote of Abraham's belief being credited to him as righteousness, he was not offering an example of someone whose faith lacked works, or faithfulness. The intent was to present Abraham as the human father of all God's children, whether Jew or Gentile (Romans 4: 16-18). His focus on justification through faith served to explain God's graceful inclusion of Gentiles in the covenant of grace who, apart from the Mosaic Law, should be accepted equally as Abraham's descendants. These verses appear in a discussion that covers nearly three chapters on this topic (Romans 2: 12- 4: 25).

Paul explained to the Jews in Rome that Abraham was credited with righteousness before circumcision and the Mosaic Law were even introduced. God's recognition of righteousness in Abraham was a matter of his faith in God. While circumcision was later given as a sign of the Abrahamic covenant, it had no bearing on God's relationship with people outside the Jewish nation or the means by which an individual might be saved. Consequently, spiritually speaking, Gentile believers are also Abraham's descendants from God's perspective.

Select passages, such as this one from Romans, are often mistakenly regarded as Paul's entire message about a person's reconciliation to God (salvation). Yet, with these words to the church in Rome (chapters 2-4), Paul was not offering direction about *how* to become a Christian. He was simply challenging the claim that Gentiles must first submit to Jewish customs and laws in order to be saved. James Coffman (1905-2006) addressed this with sound reasoning. Additionally, impressive insight is offered concerning Paul's comment about justification in *Zondervan Illustrated Bible Backgrounds Commentary.*

> **When ...** is the big word in these verses, the time of Abraham's justification being the entire basis of Paul's reasoning to the effect that Gentile converts should not be subjected either to Moses' law or the rite of circumcision, the logic of thus relaxing such requirements being in the fact of Abraham's

justification before either was in existence. This thought is the overriding consideration throughout this chapter. Such an extraneous thing as how an alien sinner is converted does not enter the consideration here in any manner.[5]

Paul...uses the verb *dikaioō* ("to justify") to refer to the establishment of a right relationship with God in this life. James...uses the language of justification in the typical Old Testament/Jewish manner to refer to what we would call the judgment... James cites Abraham to show that true faith is always revealed in deeds, and that these deeds are taken into consideration by God in the judgment.[6]

Abraham's faithful relationship with God, which was credited to him as righteousness, preceded the institutions of circumcision and the Mosaic Law. These were specific to the Abrahamic covenant as it pertained to the Jewish nation. A Gentile's relationship with God was not dependent on such things and the Jews were in no position to place a requirement upon the Gentiles that, according to Scripture, did not apply to them.

James was not addressing the same topic as Paul, which explains why his words do not contradict Paul's words to the Romans. James wrote about faith, not just in terms of sentient thought (belief only), but in terms of action (a life faithfully lived). He wrote that it is the person who seeks to honor God with his/her life who is living a life of faith.

James's approach was different from the Apostle Paul in the texts cited here. He focused on life choices and the manner in which an individual honors or dishonors God in his decisions and actions. According to James, a person who embodies the faith that is taught in

---

[5] Coffman, James B., *James Burton Coffman Commentaries, Volume VI: Romans*, ACU Press, Houston, 1984, p. 153.
[6] Arnold, Clinton E., editor, *Zondervan Illustrated Bible Backgrounds Commentary, Volume 4: Hebrews to Revelation*, Zondervan, Grand Rapids, 2002, p. 102

God's Word will offer more than false piety when it comes to filling the needs of a brother or sister in Christ.

The Greek word *erga*, which is generally translated into English as *works*, can also be translated into the English words: *actions* or *deeds*. This occurs numerous times in the NASV where it generally applies, not to obedience to commands, but to a person's way of life.

> And they do all their **deeds** (erga) to be noticed by *other* people; for they broaden their phylacteries and lengthen the tassels *of their garments*. (Matthew 23: 5) emphasis added

> Moses was educated in all the wisdom of the Egyptians, and he was proficient in speaking and **action** (ergois). (Acts 7: 22) emphasis added

> …in all things show yourself *to be* an example of good **deeds** (ergōn), *with* purity in doctrine, dignified. (Titus 2: 7) emphasis added

> [11] For this is the message which you have heard from the beginning, that we are to love one another; [12] not as Cain, *who* was of the evil one and murdered his brother. And for what reason did he murder him? Because his *own* **deeds** (erga) were evil, but his brother's were righteous. (1 John 3: 11-12) emphasis added

The examples James has offered when explaining the relationship between faith and works speak to the manner in which the believer lives life. In each decision an individual faces, they can choose to honor God, but they can also choose to dishonor God. According to James, the person of faith will choose to honor God, which is a reflection of salvific faith. That is not to say that a faithful person will never err. Indeed, people tend to err – even people of faith. Nonetheless, the person who has attained the faith of the gospel will seek to honor God in his/her decisions and actions. Those who have no inclination to honor God in their actions do not share in the faith of which Scripture speaks.

## Abraham's Faith

The reason James was comfortable using Abraham as an example is that this was a man who was fully engaged in his relationship with God. His faith in God was exhibited in his decisions and actions. By the time Abraham's belief was *credited to him as righteousness*, he had already spent decades in faithful obedience to God (cf. Genesis 12-14). His life not only reflected his faith, but he had shown himself to be God's *most faithful servant* in the entire earth. Contrary to the spurious teaching of modern theology, it was not a matter of Abraham believing God at a single moment in time and being deemed righteous in God's eyes as a result.

Similarly, in the book of Hebrews, among the Old Testament men and women who were respected for their faithfulness (Hebrews 11), the author recognized that their *belief* in God did not stand on its own. It was accompanied by and completed through their life decisions. Their decisions, or actions, were as much a part of faith as their belief in God.

This was James's point with respect to Abraham. Had Abraham lacked the faith to honor God with his life decisions, including his willingness to sacrifice his son, he would have lacked the faith God expected from him. He would have lacked the faith for which he was regarded as righteous. To Abraham's credit, his decisions and actions honored God. The same was true of each of the Old Testament faithful mentioned in the book of Hebrews.

On the Day of Pentecost, three thousand people were baptized into Christ. Afterward, according to Luke, "They were continually devoting themselves to the apostles' teaching and to fellowship, to the breaking of bread and to prayer" (Acts 2: 42). Without providing the intimate details of each person's life, Luke made the point that they lived their lives in a manner that reflected their desire to honor God and the sacrifice Jesus had made. This is the kind of work (how a person conducts his/her life) that is in view in the book of James.

People often view faith as something that is intangible. Yet, salvific faith – the faith of the gospel – is quite tangible. It is *seen* in the lives of the faithful. The actions of the Old Testament individuals mentioned in Hebrews are not only defined *as* faithful deeds, but they serve as the very *depiction* of faith. These examples were given so that believers in the first century and beyond could know what faith looks like from God's perspective.

# Chapter Five
# Paul on Faith and Works

## Paul vs Paul

It is fascinating, and even mystifying, that so many in the world of Christendom who emphasize redemption through *faith alone* seek to pit the writings of James against the works of the Apostle Paul; yet these same people fail to recognize this seeming contradiction within Paul's own words. In fact, Paul taught with eloquence the same lessons concerning faith and works found in the book of James.

There are two distinct aspects to Paul's thoughts on faith and works and it is important to distinguish between them. As noted in the previous chapter, the apostle spent much time fighting the teaching from Jewish zealots that Gentiles must first convert to Judaism before they could be recognized as Christ's followers. In that vein, when referring to works, Paul often used the phrase *works of the law*. This approach is seen in the following passages.

> [20]...by **the works of the Law** none of mankind will be justified in His sight; for through the Law *comes* knowledge of sin...[27]Where then is boasting? It has been excluded. By what kind of law? Of works? No, but by a law of faith. [28]For we maintain that a person is justified by faith apart from **works of the Law**. (Romans 3: 20, 27-28) emphasis added

> [2]Nevertheless, knowing that a person is not justified by **works of the Law** but through faith in Christ Jesus, even we have believed in Christ Jesus, so that we may be justified by faith in Christ and not by **works of the Law**; since by **works of the Law** no flesh will be justified...[5]So then, does He who provides you with the Spirit and works miracles among you, do it by **works of the Law**, or by hearing with faith?...[10]For all who

are of **works of the Law** are under a curse; for it is written: "CURSED IS EVERYONE WHO DOES NOT ABIDE BY ALL THE THINGS WRITTEN IN THE BOOK OF THE LAW, TO DO THEM." (Galatians 3: 2, 5, 10) emphasis added

In these settings, Paul was specifically addressing the insistence by some of the Jews that the Gentiles' relationship with God must go *through* Judaism. It was this very topic that sent Paul and others from Antioch to Jerusalem to consult with the apostles and elders (Acts 15: 1-11). In that council it was determined, and stated clearly, that salvation is attained through faith and that the Mosaic Law did not apply to Gentiles when it came to establishing a saving relationship with God. In fact, even where the Jews were concerned, they could consider the Law fulfilled. Paul taught that the Law had served as custodian (tutor or guardian) of God's people until the time of faith would be revealed (Galatians 3: 23-25).

The Law was fulfilled through Christ, so even the Jews should not rely on the Mosaic Law as a matter of salvation (cf. Galatians 3: 28). From a historical perspective, the Jews could never rely on the Law as a matter of salvation (cf. Romans 3: 20). The Law always looked forward to Christ as the source of redemption. Rather than invalidating the Law, faith in Christ honors the role of the Law (cf. Romans 3: 31) in that the tutorship the Law provided had proved effective for Jewish believers.

Paul touched on the Mosaic Law in certain other passages where the Romans and Galatians were concerned (cf. Romans 6: 14; 7: 1-14; Galatians 4: 21; 5: 1-4, 18). He also wrote briefly concerning "…the ministry of death, engraved in letters on stone" (2 Corinthians 3: 7), in his second letter to the church in Corinth. In these settings, he was dealing more with the believer's *relationship* to the Law in comparison to faith. These passages were not specifically about *works*.

## Not of Works

While Paul did, at times, address the challenges presented by Jewish zealots, on occasion he also wrote, outside the framework of the Mosaic Law, that salvation was a matter of faith rather than works, and these passages must not be overlooked. These include passages like his following words to the Ephesians as well as Timothy and Titus.

> [8] For by grace you have been saved through faith; and this *is* not of yourselves, *it is* the gift of God; [9] not a result of **works** (ergōn), so that no one may boast. (Ephesians 2: 8-9) emphasis added

> [8] ...but join with *me* in suffering for the gospel according to the power of God, [9] who saved us and called us with a holy calling, not according to our **works** (erga), but according to His own purpose and grace, which was granted to us in Christ Jesus from all eternity (2 Timothy 1: 8b-9) emphasis added

> He saved us, not on the basis of **deeds** (ergōn) which we did in righteousness, but in accordance with His mercy, by the washing of regeneration and renewing by the Holy Spirit. (Titus 3: 5) emphasis added

Many have singled out passages like these to serve as proof texts, insisting that they represent Paul's complete message when it comes to the relationship between faith and works. The expression "not...works" is echoed as a rallying cry, insisting that Paul was denying, and even condemning, any teaching about a relationship between faith and works where salvation was concerned, but that was not Paul's intent.

In modern times (beginning with the Reformation Movement of the sixteenth century), the concept of biblical faith has been redefined. Most view the idea of faith strictly in terms of sentient thought. In other words, *thought* equals *faith*. This, however, is not how the biblical authors portray faith.

Despite the multitude of voices claiming that Paul sought to completely divorce faith and works, his teachings are in full agreement with these other biblical authors. He taught openly that a person's faith in God is not only reflected in, but brought to fruition through, his/her actions. In words that are often overlooked in his letters to the Romans and Galatians, Paul recognized a connection between *doing* what is good in God's eyes and receiving an eternal reward. Additionally, Paul wrote to the Philippians of the importance of conduct that is in keeping with the faith of the gospel.

> [5] But because of your stubbornness and unrepentant heart you are storing up wrath for yourself on the day of wrath and revelation of the righteous judgment of God, [6] who WILL REPAY EACH PERSON ACCORDING TO HIS DEEDS: [7] to those who by perseverance in doing good seek glory, honor, and immortality, *He will give* eternal life. (Romans 2: 5-7)

> Let's not become discouraged in doing good, for in due time we will reap, if we do not become weary. (Galatians 6: 9)

> [27] Only conduct yourselves in a manner worthy of the gospel of Christ, so that whether I come and see you or remain absent, I will hear about you that you are standing firm in one spirit, with one mind striving together for the faith of the gospel. (Philippians 1: 27)

For centuries, Paul has been lauded for his teaching of *faith without works,* where the primary focus of this praise is *absence of works.* Those who applaud this teaching seem to have missed the apostle's instructions about the intimate connection between faith and works that is well-established in his epistles. He displayed fully his perspective on active faith in his introduction in the book of Romans.

> First, I thank my God through Jesus Christ for you all, because your faith is being proclaimed throughout the world. (Romans 1: 8)

It would be an impressive feat if the *thoughts* of the Christians in Rome were being "proclaimed throughout the world." After all, who could actually know their innermost thoughts? It should be obvious that Paul was not referring to their beliefs (alone). In fact, he was specifically pointing to their deeds – identifying their actions *as* their faith. It was their works that were being proclaimed. Paul drew no distinction between belief and actions where the Romans were concerned – the faith of the believer being comprised of both.

Where faith is concerned, beliefs and actions are complementary, not independent. One does not exist without the other any more than a marriage consists of a single individual. That is to say, faith naturally translates into actions. In the English language, *faith* is often viewed strictly as a mental exercise. That is because no verb form for faith exists. The idea that comes closest is *faithful*, or *faithfulness*. As noted earlier, Paul often wrote about faith in Christ in those terms (cf. 1 Corinthians 4: 17; Ephesians 1: 1; 6: 21; Colossians 1: 2, 7; 4: 7; 1 Timothy 3: 11; 2 Timothy 2: 2; Titus 1: 9).

## Obedience

The Apostle Paul is often credited with the doctrine of faith only. In fact, he is often credited with the catchphrase *faith only* – an expression that does not appear anywhere in his letters or teachings. On the other hand, Paul is rarely credited with the terms *obey, obedient, obedience,* etc., each of which appears in his writings, quite often in connection with one's response to the gospel.

> For I will not presume to speak of anything except what Christ has accomplished through me, resulting in the **obedience** of the Gentiles by word and deed. (Romans 15: 18). emphasis added

<sup>16</sup> Do you not know that *the one* to whom you present yourselves *as* slaves for **obedience**, you are slaves of *that same one* whom you **obey**, either of sin resulting in death, or of **obedience** resulting in righteousness? <sup>17</sup> But thanks be to God that though you were slaves of sin, you became **obedient** from the heart to *that* form of teaching to which you were entrusted, <sup>18</sup> and after being freed from sin, you became slaves to righteousness. (Romans 6: 16-18) emphasis added

… dealing out retribution to those who do not know God, and to those who do not **obey** the gospel of our Lord Jesus. (2 Thessalonians 1: 8) emphasis added

The topic of obedience will be addressed in greater detail in Chapter Seven, but there is no mistaking Paul's position here. It has been the practice of some in the evangelical community to misidentify *obedience* as *works*. In doing so, they have failed to appreciate the message found in these verses. With these words, Paul established a direct connection between obedience (in both word and deed) and salvation. *Obeying the gospel* is apostolic language for following biblical instruction when responding to the gospel. This can only mean that, from an apostolic perspective, *obeying* the precepts of the gospel cannot be characterized as *works*.

## The Walk of Faith

Paul furthered his teaching concerning faithfulness, or active faith, when writing to the Ephesians, Colossians, and Thessalonians. His point in the following verses is that faith and faithfulness are one. Where there is no faithfulness, there is no faith.

<sup>1</sup> Therefore I, the prisoner of the Lord, urge you to walk in a manner worthy of the calling with which you have been called, <sup>2</sup> with all humility and gentleness, with patience, bearing with one another in love, <sup>3</sup> being diligent to keep the unity of the Spirit in the bond of peace. (Ephesians 4: 1-3)

<sup>9</sup> For this reason we also, since the day we heard *about it*, have not ceased praying for you and asking that you may be filled with the knowledge of His will in all spiritual wisdom and understanding, <sup>10</sup> so that you will walk in a

manner worthy of the Lord, to please *Him* in all respects, bearing fruit in every good work and increasing in the knowledge of God; [11] strengthened with all power, according to His glorious might, for the attaining of all perseverance and patience; joyously. (Colossians 1: 9-11)

[11] just as you know how *we were* exhorting and encouraging and imploring each one of you as a father *would* his own children, [12] so that you would walk in a manner worthy of the God who calls you into His own kingdom and glory. (1 Thessalonians 2: 11-13)

With slightly different wording, Paul has taught here the very lesson offered by James. A person of faith will walk as a person of faith. The person of faith will bear fruit as they work diligently for God. The idea of walking represents action. It is the individual who perseveres patiently and joyously in their walk with God who is living the call to be a person of faith.

This walk with God is what Paul had in view as he was attempting to explain Christianity to King Agrippa while a prisoner in Caesarea. He told Agrippa:

[19] "For that reason, King Agrippa, I did not prove disobedient to the heavenly vision, [20] but *continually* proclaimed to those in Damascus first, and in Jerusalem, and *then* all the region of Judea, and *even* to the Gentiles, that they are to repent and turn to God, **performing deeds consistent with repentance**." (Acts 26: 19-20) emphasis added

The walk to which Paul has directed the believers is discussed at length in the Apostle John's first epistle where he describes it as "walking in the light" (1 John 1: 7). The theme of walking in the light, where God is identified as the light (1 John 1: 5), serves as the focus of John's letter. The idea is that as an individual navigates his/her way through this life, that person's actions should be guided using biblical instruction as the map. It will help that individual to remain in the light where stumbling blocks to a journey of faith can be avoided (John 11: 9-10).

## Not *of* Works, But *for* Works

A primary text upon which *faith only* teachers rely heavily is found in Paul's letter to the Ephesians. It is a passage that was mentioned a bit earlier, but it is a passage that deserves additional consideration since most people fail to take into account the fulness of Paul's message.

> [8]"For by grace you have been saved through faith; and this *is* not of yourselves, *it is* the gift of God; [9] not a result of works, so that no one may boast" (Ephesians 2: 8-9).

Many in the evangelical community seem to focus on these two verses as though that is where Paul's lesson begins and ends. Yet, there is much more to this passage than these two verses. When Paul wrote *not...of works*, he was not dissociating faith and works. The very next verse of the text, where works are described as a natural part of a person's walk with God, refutes that notion.

> For we are His workmanship, created in Christ Jesus for good works, which God prepared beforehand so that we would walk in them. (Ephesians 2: 10)

God's plan, as established in the gospel message, is that those who believe in Christ's sacrifice for sin have the opportunity to be made righteous in God's eyes (cf. Romans 5: 19; 2 Corinthians 5: 21; Philippians 3: 9).

> **According to Paul. The purpose of salvation through faith is to re-establish the believer in God's original plan.**

In other words, through faith, God restores the believer to the position and relationship with God that was intended when humanity was created. According to Paul, the purpose of salvation through faith is to re-establish the believer in God's original plan where mankind was created to perform good works. While the believer is saved through faith, he is saved so that he may do those works of faith that honor God.

In his letters, Paul did not differentiate between *having faith* and *being faithful*. To the apostle, there was no difference. Consequently, when Paul wrote of salvation through faith, he recognized that saving faith not only *involves* faithfulness…it *is* faithfulness. Yet, he made clear to his readers that the good works an individual performs as a matter of faith do not and cannot *earn* that person a place in heaven. If works were a *means* of entrance into the kingdom, an individual could boast that they had attained salvation on their own, negating the significance of Jesus' sacrifice. Nonetheless, the claim that one can be saved through faith alone (absent faithfulness) is as foreign to the works of Paul as it is to the writings of James.

# Chapter Six
# Jesus on Faith and Works

## Acts of Faith

Adam Clarke wrote that faith is conviction that is powerful enough for something to stand on (subsistence). Where faith in God is concerned, that conviction serves to support life decisions and a person's walk with God. Given Clarke's clarity on this topic it may help, when reading about faith within the pages of Scripture, to mentally picture the word conviction (parenthetically) following the word faith, since this is the idea that the word represents. This is the lesson learned from James, Paul, and the author of the book of Hebrews. This truth is also seen in some episodes in Jesus' life that made their way into the pages of Scripture.

The gospel writers confirmed the faith (conviction) of certain individuals as they wrote of Jesus' personal encounters. In doing so, they recognized the active character of faith. One such act of faith is seen in the story of some men who brought their paralyzed friend to Jesus (Mark 2: 3-5). When they arrived at the house where Jesus was, they could not reach him because of the crowd. Refusing to give up, they removed part of the roof and lowered their friend to Jesus. Mark wrote concerning this, "And Jesus, seeing their faith, said to the paralyzed man, 'Son, your sins are forgiven'" (Mark 2: 5).

This episode speaks to the tangible character of faith that was discussed earlier. Jesus did not need to search these men's *thoughts* to determine their measure of faith. He saw their faith in their actions. They were convinced that Jesus could heal their friend and acted in accordance with their conviction. This is the very definition of faith provided by the author of Hebrews. Their belief in Christ served as the foundation for their actions (cf. Hebrews 11: 1).

A similar episode involved a woman who had been suffering with a hemorrhaging issue for twelve years (Mark 5: 25-34). She believed Jesus could heal her of her condition, but she was evidently shy about approaching him. According to Mark, she told herself, "If I just touch his garments, I will get well" (Mark 5: 28). This woman must have been physically weak, given her condition, and the crowds pressed around Jesus. Still, her faith was such that she fought through the crowds and touched his cloak and was immediately healed from her affliction.

When Jesus felt that some of his healing power had been released, he looked around for the woman. While she was undoubtedly ecstatic that she had been healed, she was concerned that she had been discovered. Jesus comforted her fears telling her, "Daughter, your faith has made you well" (Mark 5: 34a). This is another case where the combination of a person's beliefs and actions were recognized as faith. There are many other episodes including an incident involving a man named Jairus, whose twelve-year-old daughter was dying (Luke 8: 41-42, 49-56) and a man whose son was possessed by an evil spirit (Mark 9: 17-27). In each case, faith was seen in the combination of belief and action.

> ...Jesus felt that some of his healing power had been released

## The Sermon on the Mount

Where faith is concerned, perhaps no passage of Scripture addresses the interdependence of belief and action more effectively than Jesus' words in what is known as *The Sermon on the Mount* (Matthew 5-7). Over the course of three chapters in the book of Matthew, Jesus talked about what it meant to have a relationship with God. He taught about living lives that honor God. For instance, in the beatitudes at the beginning of the sermon (Matthew 5: 3-12) he expressed the need for the disciples to be gentle (v. 5), merciful (v. 7) and peacemakers (v. 9).

Moving deeper into his sermon, Jesus challenged his listeners to perform good works that reflect their walk of faith. He told them, "Your light must shine before people in such a way that they may see your good works, and glorify your Father who is in heaven" (Matthew 5: 16). This remark demonstrates the integral role of works in the life of a person of faith.

Jesus not only addressed good works in his sermon but, in the fifth chapter of Matthew he also talked about things that dishonor God – things that have no place in the life of a believer – including anger (vv. 21-26), lust (vv. 27-28), adultery/divorce (vv. 31-32), lying (vv. 33-37), revenge (vv. 38-42), and hate (vv. 43-48).

In the second segment of his sermon, starting early in the sixth chapter of Matthew, Jesus dealt with hypocrisy in terms of how his listeners should place their beliefs into practice (v. 1). He warned them to be cautious in their deeds, explaining that they should not seek the praise of men as they serve as God's representatives on earth. In this discussion, he specifically highlighted hypocrisy in charitable giving

(vv. 2-4) and prayer (vv. 5-8) and fasting (vv. 16-18) – areas of vulnerability where someone might be tempted to put on a show.

Jesus continued in the sixth chapter, teaching the disciples about prayer, offering the Lord's Prayer as an example of godly prayer (vv. 9-13). He also spoke of the need for believers to make forgiveness of others a fundamental part of their walk (vv. 14-15). In addition, he emphasized the importance of giving (vv. 19-24) and the futility of worrying (vv. 25-34).

## Doing God's Will

In the seventh chapter of Matthew, which is the final chapter of the sermon, Jesus warned against being judgmental. After all, if someone is judgmental toward others, that person risks being hypocritical since no one is sinless. According to Jesus, the scale by which a person judges others will serve as the scale by which his own life will be measured (vv. 1-5).

After introducing things like how to approach God (vv. 7-11), the golden rule (v. 12), and the wide gate that leads to destruction contrasted against the narrow gate that leads to life (vv. 13-14), Jesus switched to a disturbing topic. He began discussing false teachers and false doctrine (vv. 15-20). In that vein, he quickly dispelled the notion that faith could be considered distinct from faithfulness with a chilling narrative.

[21] "Not everyone who says to Me, 'Lord, Lord,' will enter the kingdom of heaven, but the one who does the will of My Father who is in heaven *will enter*. [22] Many will say to Me on that day, 'Lord, Lord, did we not prophesy in Your name, and in Your name cast out demons, and in Your name perform many miracles?' [23] And then I will declare to them, 'I never knew you; LEAVE ME, YOU WHO PRACTICE LAWLESSNESS.' (Matthew 7: 21-23)

These words from Jesus are some of the most unsettling in the entire Bible. Here, in what can only be described as a heartbreaking depiction of what is to come at the time of final judgment, Jesus asked his listeners to envision a hypothetical scenario involving Judgment Day.

In that scenario, he rebuked some people who believed they were saved. In fact, they seemed to have great confidence in their walk with God. Yet, they were plainly among those who said, "Lord, Lord" and, having done so, wrongly regarded themselves as redeemed. It is possible that they even considered themselves to be among God's elite. Given their sharp response, "did we not," it appears they were stunned, and even angry, when told that they would not receive an eternal heavenly reward.

There are a number of things to consider in unwrapping the situation described here. The first matter to be considered is the belief of these people whom Jesus saw as pseudo-Christians. Did they believe in Jesus as God's son and that he came to earth to save the lost? Did they believe in atonement through Christ's blood sacrifice? Nothing in the text suggests that they got this wrong, nor did Jesus accuse them of disbelief. They were not condemned for what they believed about Jesus. They were condemned because they did not do "the will of My Father who is in heaven" (v. 21).

The condemnation of these false disciples did not come out of the blue. Jesus led up to it. To understand the unfortunate fate of those who stood before Jesus in this setting, it is necessary to take into consideration the context in which these verses appear. They come at the end of a lengthy sermon, suggesting that they may be considered the climax of Jesus teaching, providing a summary of his instructions about the personal relationship between man and God.

Jesus' sermon consisted of detailed instructions about what God expects from his followers. Is it possible that these individuals failed to follow those instructions? Were they not merciful? Did they not pray? Did their light not shine sufficiently? Where could they have fallen short? Then again, perhaps something else is in view in these verses.

It is also important to look to the verses immediately surrounding Jesus' words. When read in context, the reader finds that these verses fall on the heels of Jesus' teaching about false teachers and fruitless discipleship. Notice that the words, "Not everyone who says to me 'Lord, Lord,' will enter" seem to flow naturally from the verses prior.

The expression *kingdom of heaven* is used primarily in Matthew's gospel. Most other times in Scripture, it is referred to as the *kingdom of God*. This terminology is used in three different senses in the New Testament. At times it refers strictly to God's heavenly, spiritual realm (cf. Matthew 8: 11; 1 Corinthians 6: 9-10; Galatians 5: 21) – that which is unseen by human eyes. Other times, this phrase points more specifically to the earthly kingdom, which most often means the church, though it can also indicate God's people in a general sense (cf. Matthew 11: 12; 13: 52; Romans 14: 17; Colossians 4: 11). Still other times, the use of this phrase seems to encompass the fullness of God's kingdom, both seen (the church) and unseen (heaven) (cf. Matthew 16: 19; John 3: 3-5; 2 Thessalonians 1: 5).

Where the *Sermon on the Mount* is concerned, Jesus' words seemed to incorporate the idea of both the earthly and heavenly realms, and that is particularly true in the scenario given in these few verses. Not only would these people fail to enter the spiritual realm, but they were never part of the earthly realm (the church).

Jesus' statement "I never knew you" (v. 23) is significant in that it indicates that those who stood before him and failed to receive their anticipated eternal reward were never actually part of the kingdom of God. This is what one derives from the original language. The Greek word *oudepote* found in this text carries the same unqualified meaning as *never* in the English language, indicative of something that *had never happened* (cf. Acts 14: 8; Romans 10: 18). In other words, Jesus had never greeted them into the kingdom.

This must have shocked them, since they seemed to think they should be considered among his most worthy disciples. Evidently something was lacking in their effort to enter the kingdom, and it stands to reason that it involved the false teaching mentioned in the verses prior.

## The Parable of the Builders

Jesus followed this section with a parable that was intended to provide further insight into the condemnation experienced by those false followers in the scenario given. He began the parable of the builders (vv. 24-27) with the word "Therefore" (Gr. *oun*), a conjunction whose purpose was to link the judgment of those just mentioned in Jesus' proposed scenario to the lessons in the parable.

The primary lesson from the parable of the builders focused on foundation, with one builder erecting his house on rock while the other built on sand. Balancing this lesson with the preceding verses where Jesus discussed false teachers, it becomes evident that the problem for these pseudo disciples was found in their doctrine. That is to say, their attempt at entry into the kingdom was founded upon false teaching. Consequently, they did not *do* what God expected from them when seeking to enter the kingdom.

It is difficult to draw another conclusion from Jesus' words. No other reasoning provides an adequate explanation for this section of Scripture. These individuals believed they were part of God's kingdom. They claimed belief in Jesus, yet they had never been a part of the kingdom since *he never knew them* (v. 23). Their failure to *do God's will* prevented them from entering the kingdom (v. 21).

What does this episode say about faith and works? After all, these people claimed to have done great works in Jesus' name. Yet, if they were never part of the kingdom, perhaps Jesus was not talking about the faith/works connection, since their works were obvious. It seems more likely that this speaks to one's obedience to the gospel, which will be discussed in detail in Chapter Seven.

**An Uncanny Likeness**

Some people would too quickly dismiss James's words concerning faith and works, insisting that the teaching is not in keeping with the New Testament theme of salvation by grace through faith that is developed in the words of Paul. Hopefully the insights that have been offered here concerning Jesus' and Paul's teachings about faith and works will help to alleviate those concerns.

If what has been said so far has failed to convince that Jesus and Paul equally taught that faith is a combination of beliefs and works, perhaps this will. There is a stunning, and undoubtedly intentional, likeness between the parable of the builders offered by Jesus at the end of his sermon (Matthew 7: 24-27) and James's take on the man who was not only a hearer of the word, but a doer (James 1: 23-25).

Quite often, when Jesus shared a parable, his goal was to reveal to his audience one or more characteristics of the kingdom of heaven. For this reason, his parables were generally introduced with the words: *The kingdom of heaven is like*. This did not happen when Jesus presented the parable of the builders. Instead, like James, he introduced his metaphor by considering a person's faithful response to the message of God's Word. Notice the parallel thoughts by Jesus and James as they each distinguished between those who are of the faith and those who are not.

[24] "**Therefore, everyone who hears these words of Mine, and acts on them**, will be like a wise man who built his house on the rock. [25] And the rain fell and the floods came, and the winds blew and slammed against that house; and *yet* it did not fall, for it had been founded on the rock. [26] **And everyone who hears these words of Mine, and does not act on them**, will be like a foolish man who built his house on the sand. (Matthew 7: 24-26) emphasis added

[23] **For if anyone is a hearer of the word and not a doer**, he is like a man who looks at his natural face in a mirror; [24] for *once* he has looked at himself and gone away, he has immediately forgotten what kind of person he was. [25] **But one who has looked intently at the perfect law**, the *law* of freedom, **and has continued *in it*, not having become a forgetful hearer but an active doer**... (James 1: 23-25) emphasis added

Measuring Jesus' words (in bold print) against those made by James (in bold print), these two passages are worthy of serious reflection. Jesus and James not only taught the same lesson concerning faith, but they effectively used the same words to make the point. James's words echo Jesus' message from *The Sermon on the Mount*. This speaks volumes when it comes to understanding the harmony that is found in the words of Jesus, James, and Paul concerning faith and works.

# Chapter Seven
# Works vs Obedience

**Conversion**

Bible scholars and laymen alike who claim Jesus as their personal savior largely agree with the teaching that there is a moment in time when an individual accepts Jesus as savior and experiences initial salvation. This is generally regarded as the time of conversion. It is that time when a person's sins are forgiven, and he/she is transformed from a state of condemnation to a redeemed state.

In the New Testament, the writers identify those who have been saved using an assortment of words and phrases. Those who had experienced conversion are identified as *reborn* (John 3: 3), *believers* (Acts 16: 34), *renewed* (Romans 6: 4), *justified* (1 Corinthians 6: 11), *attained eternal life*, (Ephesians 1: 7), *redeemed* (1 Timothy 1: 16), *forgiven* (1 John 2: 12), as well as a few other expressions. Each of the terms listed here is employed more than once to recognize those who are saved. While there is general agreement that there is a moment of conversion, doctrinal views abound when it comes to identifying that moment.

**Weighing Works and Obedience**

Paul taught plainly that no one may *earn* his/her way to heaven by performing good works, and he was unequivocal where that teaching was concerned. His words on this are readily available for all to see (cf. Ephesians 2: 8-9; 2 Timothy 1: 9; Titus 3: 5). Whether it is one deed or one thousand deeds, no amount of good works can help anyone gain access to heaven since there are no good works that rise to that level of righteousness.

While Paul taught that salvation was not a matter of *works*, he did not take that same position when it came to obedience – specifically, obedience to the gospel (cf. Romans 6: 17). This can only mean that, in the apostle's view, obedience was distinct from good works. According to Paul, a person could not reach heaven by performing good works, but neither could he reach heaven absent obedience to the gospel message. The Apostle Peter took a similar stand concerning obedience to the gospel (1 Peter 4: 17).

## Obeying the Gospel

Jesus told his disciples, "I am the way, and the truth, and the life; no one comes to the Father except through Me" (John 14: 6). The most obvious lesson from this statement is that heaven/eternal life is inaccessible to those whose sins are not cleansed by the blood of Christ. This is taught consistently throughout the pages of the New Testament (cf. Acts 20: 28; Romans 5: 9; Ephesians 1: 7; Hebrews 9: 14). Yet, Jesus' words include an additional, much more subtle lesson. That lesson is that Jesus has the right to decide *how* mankind can access that cleansing. Access to his blood is given to those who *obey the gospel*. This is in keeping with the teachings from Jesus, Peter, and Paul.

God did not leave it upon the shoulders of men to decide their own path to Jesus. The fact that people have proffered assorted claims about what constitutes the moment of conversion indicates that many have discounted biblical instruction about *how* an individual can access Christ's cleansing blood and have his/her sins washed away.

Obedience to the gospel message is the biblically prescribed manner through which a person is saved by faith. It is the faith response God wants to see from every individual who seeks salvation (cf. Acts 6: 7). This is undoubtedly what Paul had in view when he used phrases like "obedience of faith" (Romans 1: 5; 16: 26). This same lesson is conveyed in the following verses from the apostles.

> But thanks be to God that though you were slaves of sin, you became obedient from the heart to *that* form of teaching to which you were entrusted (Romans 6: 17)

> …dealing out retribution to those who do not know God, and to those who do not obey the gospel of our Lord Jesus. (2 Thessalonians 1: 8)

> …you have purified your souls in obedience to the truth… (1 Peter 1: 22)

> For *it is* time for judgment to begin with the household of God; and if *it begins* with us first, what *will be* the outcome for those who do not obey the gospel of God? (1 Peter 4: 17)

God has laid out in Scripture the measures that constitute obedience to the message of the gospel.[7] They are not burdensome steps, particularly when weighed against the eternal life

> **God has laid out…the measures that constitute obedience to the message of the gospel.**

and eternal damnation outcomes that lay in store for the obedient and the disobedient respectively. Sadly, it could be the simplicity of these

---

[7] While no single verse of Scripture displays the precepts of the gospel in full, the following passages combine to provide both Messianic and apostolic instruction concerning what God expects from those who wish to enter the kingdom: Matthew 28: 19-20; Mark 15: 15-16; John 3: 1-5, 16; Acts 2: 38; 3: 19; 11: 18; 16: 14-15, 25-34; 18: 8; 22: 16; Romans 6: 1-4; 10: 9-10; 2 Corinthians 7: 10; 9: 13; Ephesians 2: 8-9; 5: 26; 1 Peter 3: 21; Titus 3: 5; 1 John 1: 9.

steps that makes them so easy to ignore. Matthew Henry (1662-1714) wrote concerning this truth in connection with Jesus' return and the Day of Judgment in 2 Thessalonians 1: 9:

> This is the great crime of multitudes, the gospel is revealed, and they will not believe it; or if they pretend to believe, they will not obey it. Believing the truths of the gospel, is in order to our obeying the precepts of the gospel. [8]

Some may wonder if it might be considered overreach to knit *belief* and *obedience* so closely together. After all, are these not two separate issues? To a degree they are separate as is evident in the words from Matthew Henry. Yet, in the following text, when writing about those Israelites of old who were not allowed to enter the Promised Land, the author of the book of Hebrews recognized that the two matters (belief and obedience) go hand in hand. That was Mr. Henry's point. Just as faith is made complete through deeds (James 2: 22), belief is made complete through obedience.

> [18] And to whom did He swear that they would not enter His rest, but to those who were **disobedient**? [19] And *so* we see that they were not able to enter because of **unbelief**. (Hebrews 3: 18-19) emphasis added

Given the apostles' piercing words about the relationship between obedience and salvation (2 Thessalonians 1: 8; 1 Peter 4: 17), it is not unreasonable to suppose that failure to *obey* the gospel may help explain the Day of Judgment scenario that Jesus offered at the end of the *Sermon on the Mount* (Matthew 7: 21-23), which was discussed in Chapter Six. The condemnation of those pseudo disciples mentioned suggests that, in their failed effort to enter the kingdom, they ignored godly

---

[8] Henry, Matthew, *Matthew Henry's Commentary on the Whole Bible: Complete and Unabridged*, Hendrickson Publishers, Inc., Peabody, MA, p. 2346.

instructions. They had evidently tried to enter through the wide gate that "leads to destruction" (Matthew 7: 13). It is difficult to imagine another explanation that solves that mystery. Jesus seemed to make this same point later in Matthew's gospel, insisting that it is those who *do God's will* who, unlike the counterfeit followers mentioned in his sermon, are allowed to participate in the spiritual brotherhood of Christ (Matthew 12: 50).

The Bible goes far in drawing a distinction between what constitutes obedience, through which an individual enters the kingdom, and godly works that reflect a person's faith in and relationship with God. The notion that the individuals in the above-mentioned scenario had failed to obey biblical instruction in their effort to enter the kingdom is effectively addressed in these words from D. A. Carson.

> The determinative factor regarding who enters the kingdom is obedience to the Father's will (v. 19, cf. 12: 50).[9]

> Moreover, Matthew, as we shall see, strongly stresses grace; therefore it is legitimate to wonder whether he is presenting obedience to the will of the Father as the ground or as the requirement for entrance into the kingdom. Paul would deny only the former and would insist on the latter no less than Matthew would.[10]

The same foundational lesson of obedience that is displayed in connection with these self-styled disciples in the *Sermon on the Mount*, as well as in the parable of the builders that explains their dilemma, was reiterated by Paul in his first letter to the Corinthians.

> [10] According to the grace of God which was given to me, like a wise master builder I laid a foundation, and another is building on it. But each person must

---

[9] Carson, D. A., *The Expositor's Bible Commentary: Matthew*, Zondervan Publishing House, Grand Rapids, MI, 1995, p. 192
[10] Ibid, p. 193

be careful how he builds on it. [11] For no one can lay a foundation other than the one which is laid, which is Jesus Christ. (1 Corinthians 3: 10-11)

The apostles were deliberate in distinguishing between *obedience to the gospel* and *godly works*. Unfortunately, since the days of the Reformation Movement and the introduction of the *Five Solae*, those who have sought to de-emphasize the connection between *faith* and *works* have often ended up wrongly equating *works* and *obedience*. This has resulted in a lesson of salvation without obedience, in direct conflict with apostolic instruction.

The precepts of the gospel message are taught plainly and purposefully throughout the New Testament (see footnote on p. 56). It is true that any attempt to earn a place in heaven via works is futile. However, the apostles have presented obedience, not as a means of earning a place in heaven, but as the narrow gateway that "leads to life" (Matthew 7: 14). It is the pathway of faith designated by Jesus for people to access his cleansing blood. Given this distinction, it seems unwise, and spiritually perilous, to discount the high value the apostles placed upon obeying the gospel.

# Chapter Eight
# Judgment Day

## Eschatology

The human study of the end times is often referred to as *eschatology*. In biblical terms, this points to the occasion of Jesus' Second Coming and the earthly events surrounding his anticipated return. It is a challenge to attempt to sort out eschatological events that are described in God's Word. It is an even greater challenge to apply any kind of chronology to those events. There are a multitude of views about what is to come. Some of those views are steeped in Scripture. Others, not so much.

The *rapture* is a topic that has produced so many views that it is difficult to count them all, much less address them on an individual basis. Some students of Scripture decry the use of the term *rapture*, based partly on the fact that this word does not appear in English translations of Scripture. Yet, many of those same individuals have no issue with the word *trinity*, even though it does not appear in God's Word. Their explanation is that the idea of the trinity is biblically based, so the word is acceptable. Yet, it can be argued that the *idea* of a rapture is also biblically based (cf. 1 Corinthians 15: 51-53). There is no question that the day will come when "...the dead in Christ will rise first" (1 Thessalonians 4: 16) and the living will be "...caught up together in the clouds" (1 Thessalonians 4: 17). Labeling, or refusing to label that event as the *rapture* is of little consequence.

The word *rapture* comes from the Latin Vulgate (Bible) where it is rendered *rapiemur*. It was translated from the Greek *harpazo*, a form of which is used in the Thessalonians text (above), meaning *caught up*. This is how the term is generally translated into English (cf. 2 Corinthians 12: 2; Revelation 12: 5).

It seems much of the controversy over the term *rapture*, and the final judgment generally, lies in the varying views about the character of the event described in the Thessalonians text. People seem to have settled into three major camps on this point. What is most interesting is that each view has developed largely, although not solely, from the same passage of Scripture (Revelation 20: 1-6). The differences derive from assorted views about the one thousand years (millennium) mentioned in this passage. The following paragraphs highlight these assorted views in a general sense without getting too deeply involved in how those views have developed over the centuries.

One point of view is known as premillennialism, indicating that Jesus will return to rapture believers prior to the one thousand years mentioned in the text (Revelation 20: 2). According to this philosophy, the rapture will be a subtle, and even secretive event. That is to say, believers will be raptured (both dead and living), and the lost will remain behind, dumbfounded by what has occurred. The rapture will be followed by seven years of tribulation after which Christ will return a third time to begin a physical one-thousand-year reign on earth. During that time, Satan will be bound, preventing him from interfering in Christ's reign. It is the claim of a *secret* rapture, combined with a third appearance of Christ, that seems to have soured many individuals toward the use of the term *rapture*.

A second view, known as amillennialism, takes a different approach. The prefix "a" negates the literal view of the term millennium just as the term *atheist* (unbeliever) counters *theist* (believer). For the amillennialist, the reign of Christ should not be interpreted to mean that he will physically reign on earth for one thousand years. As with numerous other passages of Scripture, one thousand years is considered figurative, depicting a long period of time (cf. 2 Peter 3: 8). Nor will this reign occur after the rapture of the saints. Instead, the reign of which Scripture speaks is the church age (from Pentecost until the Day of Judgment). Satan is bound during the church age, indicating that his influence on the human race will be *limited*. The church age will end when Christ returns to judge the living and the dead.

Postmillennialism is admittedly a bit vague when compared to these other views. Like amillennialism, the one thousand years mentioned in the book of Revelation is considered figurative rather than literal. The difference is that, in postmillennialism, it is not meant to denote a *specific* period of time. According to this view, the idea of the millennium represents a phase when God's kingdom will realize its fullness here on earth as Satan is bound and, thus, prevented from influencing humanity. During the millennium, mankind will experience a godly, peaceful, and prosperous world as Christianity abounds. At the end of this time frame, Christ will return to judge humanity. Regardless of the position an individual may take on these various *isms*, everyone seems to agree on one point. Judgment Day is coming.

## The Design of Judgment Day

Setting aside millennial views, it might be interesting to consider what Judgment Day will look like. After all, it will be a day like no other. It seems the closest equivalent would be the days of creation. Other most significant days include the days of Jesus' birth, death, resurrection, and ascension as well as the Day of Pentecost, as the Holy Spirit was introduced to humankind and the church of Christ was established. Beyond these, nothing comes close.

Will the Judgment begin and end within twenty-four hours? It is, after all, called the Day of Judgment. It is probably unwise to get too entangled in the terminology. It certainly signifies the time of Jesus' return, but in terms of human time, the wording is likely irrelevant. According to Peter, "...with the Lord one day is like a thousand years, and a thousand years like one day" (2 Peter 3: 8). Also, the event will undoubtedly be so captivating that the passing of time will be inconsequential.

People have different perspectives on the events of the Day depending on their millennial views. For instance, some believe different people will be judged at different times, but it seems the most reasonable conclusion, based on biblical instruction, is that all of humanity will be together in one place, at least for a time. Every person who has died will be raised and everyone who is living will be transformed to a spiritual state, although it seems clear that the saved will be taken first. In other words, a first century disciple might stand shoulder to shoulder with a twenty first century minister. This teaching has been derived primarily from Jesus' words in what is generally referred to as the Olivet Discourse (Matthew 25: 31-46).

Evidently, the time of judgment will begin with "all the nations…gathered before Him" (Matthew 25: 32a). Scripture indicates that this will be the only time that all of humankind who have ever lived will be together in one place. The co-mingling of the lost and the saved will end in short order. It appears that the first order of the Day will be to "**32**…separate them from one another, just as the shepherd separates the sheep from the goats; **33** and He will put the sheep on His right, but the goats on the left" (Matthew 25: 32b-33). Once this has happened, the judgment begins.

## The Judge

The idea of a day of ultimate judgment for humankind dates back to the Old Testament where certain voices among the prophets indicated that such a day is coming. Who will sit on the throne of judgment on that day? Some passages can be a bit confusing, like those cited below.

> The men of Nineveh will stand up with this generation at the judgment and condemn it, because they repented at the preaching of Jonah; and behold, *something* greater than Jonah is here. (Luke 11: 32)

> Or do you not know that the saints will judge the world? If the world is judged by you, are you not competent *to form* the smallest law courts? (1 Corinthians 6: 2)

> And Jesus said to them, "Truly I say to you, that you who have followed Me, in the regeneration when the Son of Man will sit on His glorious throne, you also shall sit upon twelve thrones, judging the twelve tribes of Israel. (Matthew 19: 28)

Of course, *the men of Nineveh* will not serve as judge on the Day of Judgment (Luke 11: 32). Jesus has identified them here, not as judges in the conventional sense, but as a model of repentance against which others might be judged – the kind of repentance he had not seen in his current generation. Consequently, the Ninevites will serve as evidence against those whose lack of repentance will lead to their condemnation. Nor will the human "saints…judge the world" (1 Corinthians 6: 2). On this occasion, the apostle was dealing with the fact that the Corinthian believers could not seem to settle certain issues among themselves and would end up going to court. The statement concerning judgment seems to be a slight jab suggesting that they were arrogant, thinking they were of such character that they could administer justice to the world, yet they could not seem to act justly even in their own church family.

Will the apostles judge the tribes of Israel (Matthew 19: 28)? This does not appear to be what Jesus had in mind when he spoke these words. Albert Barnes (1798-1870) and James Coffman wrote concerning Jesus' remarks:

> This is figurative. To sit on a throne denotes power and honor, and means here that they would be distinguished above others, and be more highly honored and rewarded.[11]

> This was not a reference to literal thrones but to spiritual thrones of eminence and authority in Christ's kingdom, from which they should exercise influence, not over fleshly Israel but over the spiritual Israel which is the church (Romans 9:6; Galatians 3:29).[12]

The message from Scripture is clear. Final authority for the judgment of humankind rests with God the Father. This message is seen in both the Old and New Testaments.

> I said to myself, "God will judge the righteous and the wicked," for a time for every matter and for every deed is there. (Ecclesiastes 3: 17)

---

[11] Barnes, Albert, *Albert Barnes' Notes on the Whole Bible*, Matthew 19 - Albert Barnes' Notes on the Whole Bible - Bible Commentaries - StudyLight.org, accessed August 22, 2021.
[12] Coffman, James, *James Burton Coffman Commentaries, Volume I: Matthew*, ACU Press, Abilene, TX, 1984, p. 300.

If you address as Father the One who impartially judges according to each one's work, conduct yourselves in fear during the time of your stay *on earth*; (1 Peter 1: 17)

Just as God the Father holds in his hands the authority to judge mankind, he has the authority to relinquish that role, placing the judgment of humankind in the hands of his appointee. According to Scripture, he has appointed Jesus as judge. He earned that right, surrendering himself on behalf of humanity in order to provide a path to reconciliation with God. Who better to faithfully judge the world?

For not even the Father judges anyone, but He has given all judgment to the Son. (John 5: 22)

...because He has set a day on which He will judge the world in righteousness through a Man whom He has appointed, having furnished proof to all people by raising Him from the dead. (Acts 17: 31)

...on the day when, according to my gospel, God will judge the secrets of mankind through Christ Jesus. (Romans 2: 15)

These, along with other passages, testify to the fact that Jesus will serve as judge on that day. Although Jesus will sit on the judgment throne, as a member of the Godhead (Father, Son, and Holy Spirit) he will undoubtedly deliver the same justice that would be rendered by God the Father or the Holy Spirit. They think as one and they act in harmony with one another.

## The Subjects of Judgment

Who will face judgment? The answer is that every member of the human race will face Jesus in judgment. Although, a strong argument can be made that there will be exceptions for the souls of those

> ...every member of the human race will face Jesus in judgment

66

lost to abortion, miscarriage, and infant death, as well as children who passed from this life at an innocent age and those innocents who remain alive at the time of the Parousia. It is difficult to say how judgment might apply in those cases, and Scripture fails to address the subject. This is probably because that is not a concern for the rest of humanity. On the other hand, everyone who can differentiate right from wrong – those who have sinned against God – will face judgment. Some have mistakenly deduced that believers will not face the final judgment based on assorted passages of Scripture, such as those cited below.

> I, I *alone*, am the one who wipes out your wrongdoings for My own sake, And I will not remember your sins. (Isaiah 43: 25)

> None of his sins that he has committed will be remembered against him. He has practiced justice and righteousness; he shall certainly live. (Ezekiel 33: 13)

> Truly, truly, I say to you, the one who hears My word, and believes Him who sent Me, has eternal life, and does not come into judgment, but has passed out of death into life. (John 5: 24)

> FOR I WILL BE MERCIFUL TOWARD THEIR WRONGDOINGS, AND THEIR SINS I WILL NO LONGER REMEMBER. (Hebrews 8: 12)

> AND THEIR SINS AND THEIR LAWLESS DEEDS I WILL NO LONGER REMEMBER. (Hebrews 10: 17)

The verses from the Old Testament must be taken in context. In Isaiah, these words were spoken to, and refer to, the children of Israel. They cannot be applied to Gentiles. God's willingness to forget their sins was not for the sake of the Israelites, but for his own sake since he was grieved by their unfaithfulness. These words are not about the final judgment, but about God's dealings with the Israelites in this life. He was so "wearied…with your wrongdoings" (Isaiah 43: 24) that his only option was to overlook, or *erase*, their sins.

The Ezekiel text was also specific to the Israelites as God defended his own sense of justice. While this setting seems to be more in line with eternal life/death, the idea in this passage is not that the Israelites' sins would be completely forgotten, but that the righteous will live, and the unrighteous will die (spiritually speaking).

Jesus' words in John 5: 24 are a source of great confusion for many. The NASV, along with several other translations, suggests that the believer "does not come into judgement." In this case, the Greek *krisin* is probably better translated *justice*, or *condemnation*. Certain English versions use the term condemnation or condemned in this setting (i.e., CEV, KJV, NLT). The idea is that these individuals will not face the justice, or condemnation, they deserve.

The two texts from the book of Hebrews speak to the reason God established the covenant of grace. The first covenant failed to provide the means for God to forget sins. That is to say, without the new covenant, everyone would be eternally separated from God for their sins. Jesus' sacrifice through which the new covenant was established, provided the means for God to forget (cleanse) sins. Hebrews 10 says much the same thing. Thomas Constable has written concerning these verses:

> The writer proceeded to explain the superiority of the New Covenant that Jesus Christ ratified with His blood (death) that is better than the Old Mosaic Covenant that He terminated when He died. He first explained the reason for the change in covenants (Hebrews 8:6-9), then he quoted the four superior promises of the New Covenant (Hebrews 8:10-12), and finally he underlined the certainty of the change (Hebrews 8:13).[13]

---

[13] Constable, Thomas, *Expository Notes of Dr. Thomas Constable*, Hebrews 8 - Expository Notes of Dr. Thomas Constable - Bible Commentaries - StudyLight.org, accessed August 23, 2021.

The statement that God will remember sins no more (Hebrews 10:17) means that He will no longer call them back to memory with a view to condemning the sinner (cf. Romans 8:1).[14]

The point that the faithful will not be condemned for their sins is perhaps best stated in a verse referenced by Constable. Freedom from condemnation is the lesson found in the following words from Paul to the church in Rome.

Therefore there is now no condemnation at all for those who are in Christ Jesus. (Romans 8: 1)

That each individual will participate in the judgment process is well-established in both the Old and New Testaments as seen in the following passages, and that teaching does not conflict with those verses where it is stated that God would not remember sins. Paul and Peter each made a special point of explaining this to the believers. The Apostle Paul conspicuously and consistently included himself among those who will face the judgment.

I said to myself, "God will judge the righteous and the wicked," for a time for every matter and for every deed is there." (Ecclesiastes 3: 17)

[1] For we will all appear before the judgment seat of God…[12] So then each one of us will give an account of himself to God. (Romans 14: 1, 12)

For we must all appear before the judgment seat of Christ, so that each one may receive compensation for his deeds *done* through the body, in accordance with what he has done, whether good or bad. (2 Corinthians 5: 10)

…they will give an account to Him who is ready to judge the living and the dead. (1 Peter 4: 5)

---

[14] Constable, Thomas, *Expository Notes of Dr. Thomas Constable*, Hebrews 10 - Expository Notes of Dr. Thomas Constable - Bible Commentaries - StudyLight.org, accessed August 23, 2021.

# Chapter Nine
# The Judgment

## The Book of Life

Judgment, whether earthly or spiritual in nature, comes in two parts. The first phase is to determine whether someone is guilty or not guilty. In the United States judicial systems, when an individual is found not guilty, that is the end of that person's judgment. They are freed from the burden of facing further action. On the other hand, the person found guilty faces the second phase of judgment, which is determining an equitable punishment for the wrong that has been committed.

Things work a bit differently when it comes to spiritual judgment. A person's state of guilt or innocence is determined prior to facing the judge. According to Scripture, "And if anyone's name was not found written in the book of life, he was thrown into the lake of fire" (Revelation 20: 15).

The topic of the *book of life* is one that presents many challenges. This expression appears only eight times in Scripture – once in the Old Testament with the balance in the New Testament. Of the seven appearances in the New Testament, six are found in the book of Revelation. The topic is especially challenging in that it is difficult to determine if and when names might be added to or erased from the book.

> May they be wiped out of the **book of life**, And may they not be recorded with the righteous. (Psalm 69: 28) emphasis added

Indeed, true companion, I ask you also, help these women who have shared my struggle in *the cause of* the gospel, together with Clement as well as the rest of my fellow workers, whose names are in the **book of life**. (Philippians 4: 3) emphasis added

The one who overcomes will be clothed the same way, in white garments; and I will not erase his name from the **book of life**, and I will confess his name before My Father and before His angels. (Revelation 3: 5) emphasis added

All who live on the earth will worship him, *everyone* whose name has not been written since the foundation of the world in the **book of life** of the Lamb who has been slaughtered. (Revelation 13: 8) emphasis added

The beast that you saw was, and is not, and is about to come up out of the abyss and go to destruction. And those who live on the earth, whose names have not been written in the **book of life** from the foundation of the world, will wonder when they see the beast, that he was, and is not, and will come. (Revelation 17: 8) emphasis added

And I saw the dead, the great and the small, standing before the throne, and books were opened; and another book was opened, which is *the **book** of life*; and the dead were judged from the things which were written in the books, according to their deeds. (Revelation 20: 12) emphasis added

And if anyone's name was not found written in the **book of life**, he was thrown into the lake of fire. (Revelation 20: 15) emphasis added

nothing unclean, and no one who practices abomination and lying, shall ever come into it, but only those whose names are written in the Lamb's **book of life**. (Revelation 21: 27) emphasis added

Certain passages (Psalm 69: 28; Revelation 3: 5) suggest that names can be erased from (and perhaps added to) the book of life. Yet, two passages (Revelation 13: 8; 17: 8) indicate that at least some names in that book were determined and written at or before "the foundation of the world." Since the only information provided in Scripture is found in the verses listed above, it seems there is little to be gained from dwelling too heavily on the complex nature of that book. It is a book designed for spiritual eyes only.

For those who may be concerned that God predetermined who would be saved, since names were written "from the foundation of the world," this should not be cause for alarm.

> ...God has known from the beginning who will receive an eternal heavenly reward.

It is true that God has known from the beginning who will receive an eternal heavenly reward. However, *knowing* a result is not the same as *determining* a result. God is omniscient (cf. Psalm 147: 5; Hebrews 4: 13; 1 John 3: 20). Consequently, he has known from the beginning the decisions individuals will make and the identities of believers. That does not mean that he has *decided* who would believe. A person's freewill choice to follow Christ is taught forthrightly in Gods' Word (cf. Mark 8: 34; Romans 10: 9-10; 2 Peter 3: 9).

What Scripture does say is that the names of the saved are recorded in the book of life. It does not matter when they were included in the book. The only critical factor for each individual is whether his/her name is included in the book either at that person's time of death or, for those who remain alive at the Parousia, at the time of judgment.

## The Sheep and the Goats

The first order of business on that day will be the separation of the sheep (the saved) from the goats (the lost) (Matthew 25: 32-33). The saved will be moved to the right side of the throne while the lost will be placed on the left. Note also that deciding who is saved is not a subjective decision on Jesus' part (cf. 1 Peter 1: 17). The saved/lost state of each individual will be made prior to this time. Those whose names appear in the book of life will be placed on the right side of the throne.

Whose names will be written in the book of life? It will be those who are of the faith. How will Jesus decide who is of the faith and who is not? According to Scripture, the saved are those who have responded faithfully to the gospel message presented in God's Word – those whose sins have been cleansed by Christ's blood. In that sense, it is up to each individual whether his/her name appears there.

There will be many who, during their lifetime, never had the opportunity to hear the message of the gospel. How will their eternal fate be determined? Certainly, it will be an objective rather than a subjective judgment. The saved/lost state of each person will be grounded in his/her response to God based on the information available. How each one responds to God will determine that person's eternal fortune. This is true of all those who died prior to the Day of Pentecost when the message of the gospel was formally proclaimed to humankind as well as those who, after that day, died without hearing of Christ.

## The Second Phase of Judgment

The difference between judgment in a human court of law and the spiritual judgment on the Day of the Lord is that on earth, when a *not guilty* verdict is rendered, that is the end of that person's trial. On Judgment Day, the saved – those whom Jesus has determined are no longer guilty of their sins since their sins have been cleansed by his blood – face an additional phase when it comes to eternal judgment.

The punishment for the lost is declared plainly in God's Word. "And if anyone's name was not found written in the book of life, he was thrown into the lake of fire" (Revelation 20: 15). While this seems to be a straightforward declaration, it is arguable that even this proclamation is not as constricting as the wording suggests.

The Bible teaches that every person, whether saved or lost, will be required to stand before the throne and give account for the life he/she has lived. This is true of everyone, whether they stand on the right or left side of the throne, and it is a message that is well-established in both testaments.

> [13] The conclusion, when everything has been heard, *is*: fear God and keep His commandments, because this *applies to* every person. [14] For God will bring every act to judgment, everything which is hidden, whether it is good or evil. (Ecclesiastes 12: 13-14)

> But there is nothing covered up that will not be revealed, and hidden that will not be known. (Luke 12: 2)

> Therefore do not go on passing judgment before *the* time, *but wait* until the Lord comes, who will both bring to light the things hidden in the darkness and disclose the motives of *human* hearts; and then praise will come to each person from God. (1 Corinthians 4: 5)

> And just as it is destined for people to die once, and after this *comes* judgment. (Hebrews 9: 27)

Giving account for the actions that constitute a person's life in the flesh is a phase of judgment that applies to everyone, not just the lost. Those actions for which people will give account include both good and evil deeds. This clarifies the meaning behind certain verses where God proclaimed that he would remember sins no more. The meaning is that those sins would not be held against an individual when it comes to determining his/her eternal state – that is, whether a person will be among the sheep or the goats.

On the Day of Judgment, different books will be opened. Along with the book of life, John indicates that other books will be opened. It is difficult to say, but it could be that the dead mentioned in the following verse is a reference to the lost and does not refer to those who stand on the right side of the throne.

> And I saw the dead, the great and the small, standing before the throne, and books were opened; and another book was opened, which is *the book* of life; and the dead were judged from the things which were written in the books, according to their deeds. (Revelation 20: 12)

Whether these books contain the deeds of every man or a set of righteous standards by which those deeds are measured is difficult to say since that is not revealed. Still, it is the contents of these books by which men will be judged as they face the consequences of their decisions and actions while in the flesh.

## Judging the Lost

It is impossible for humankind, while in the flesh, to imagine the spiritual world with any sense of clarity. Nonetheless, it is clear that the lost, having been judged, will be "thrown into the lake of fire" (Revelation 20: 15). Before that happens, each one will be required to give account for his deeds, but to what end?

If all of the lost will be cast into the lake of fire, what logic can be applied for reviewing each one's deeds, whether good or evil? Some have stated that part of the reason for this is so that God can provide evidence that his judgment is just. That could certainly be part of the reason, but the following verses suggest that something else may also be in play.

> I, the LORD, search the heart, I test the mind,
> To give to each person according to his ways,
> According to the results of his deeds. (Jeremiah 17: 10)

> [36] But I tell you that *for* every careless word that people speak, they will give an account of it on *the* day of judgment. [37] For by your words you will be justified, and by your words you will be condemned. (Matthew 12: 36-37)

75

For the Son of Man is going to come in the glory of His Father with His angels, and WILL THEN REPAY EVERY PERSON ACCORDING TO HIS DEEDS. (Matthew 16: 27)

[5] But because of your stubbornness and unrepentant heart you are storing up wrath for yourself on the day of wrath and revelation of the righteous judgment of God, [6] who WILL REPAY EACH PERSON ACCORDING TO HIS DEEDS: (Romans 2: 5-6)

Therefore it is not surprising if his servants also disguise themselves as servants of righteousness, whose end will be according to their deeds. (2 Corinthians 11: 15)

If you address as Father the One who impartially judges according to each one's work, conduct yourselves in fear during the time of your stay *on earth* (1 Peter 1: 17)

…and I will give to each one of you according to your deeds. (Revelation 2: 23)

[12]…and the dead were judged from the things which were written in the books, according to their deeds. [13]And the sea gave up the dead who were in it, and Death and Hades gave up the dead who were in them; and they were judged, each one *of them* according to their deeds. (Revelation 20: 12b-13)

Salvation is a matter of grace through faith in Jesus' sacrifice of atonement. This is an objective judgment as it is those who, through faithful obedience to the gospel, will be saved. Yet, the expression *according to deeds*, which is repeated time and again in Scripture, seems to suggest a sense of proportionality when it comes to meting out justice. This has nothing to do with whether a person is lost or saved, but perhaps it speaks to rendering degrees of punishment where the lost are concerned.

There are those among the lost who will have lived their lives without giving the gospel message honest consideration, uninterested in Jesus' sacrifice for their sins. Yet, many of those same people will have cared for their fellowman, provided for the poor, and performed many other good works.

On the other hand, some will have spent their time on earth not only hating God but living their lives in hostile defiance of his purpose. Will the members of these groups receive exactly the same eternal sentence? Certain passages of Scripture suggest that there may well be varying degrees of punishment for the lost.

> [21] "Woe to you, Chorazin! Woe to you, Bethsaida! For if the miracles that occurred in you had occurred in Tyre and Sidon, they would have repented long ago in sackcloth and ashes. [22] Nevertheless I say to you, it will be more tolerable for Tyre and Sidon on *the* day of judgment than for you. [23] And you, Capernaum, will not be exalted to heaven, will you? You will be brought down to Hades! For if the miracles that occurred in you had occurred in Sodom, it would have remained to this day. [24] Nevertheless I say to you that it will be more tolerable for the land of Sodom on *the* day of judgment, than for you." Matthew 11: 21-24)

> [47] And that slave who knew his master's will and did not get ready or act in accordance with his will, will receive many blows, [48] but the one who did not know *it*, and committed acts deserving of a beating, will receive *only* a few blows. From everyone who has been given much, much will be demanded; and to whom they entrusted much, of him they will ask all the more. (Luke 12: 47-48)

> [26] For if we go on sinning willfully after receiving the knowledge of the truth, there no longer remains a sacrifice for sins, [27] but a terrifying expectation of judgment and THE FURY OF A FIRE WHICH WILL CONSUME THE ADVERSARIES. [28] Anyone who has ignored the Law of Moses is put to death without mercy on *the testimony of* two or three witnesses. [29] How much more severe punishment do you think he will deserve who has trampled underfoot the Son of God, and has regarded as unclean the blood of the covenant by which he was sanctified, and has insulted the Spirit of grace? [30] For we know Him who said, "VENGEANCE IS MINE, I WILL REPAY." And again, "THE LORD WILL JUDGE HIS PEOPLE." [31] It is a terrifying thing to fall into the hands of the living God. (Hebrews 10: 26-31)

It will be better to be among the sheep on the Day of Judgment rather than the goats and it is unlikely that receiving a lesser punishment will offer much consolation. Still, it seems there is a possibility that, being judged according to deeds, the lost may be sentenced to varying levels of eternal punishment.

## Rewarding the Saved

While the lost may face grades of punishment when it comes to their eternal fortunes, there is far more evidence indicating that the saved will experience gradations of rewards, or blessings, in the hereafter. Some of this is seen in passages that have already been mentioned (cf. Matthew 16: 27; Revelation 2: 23). Additionally, the parable of the talents suggests strongly that rewards will be based on how individuals have served God while on earth (Matthew 25: 14-30).

Heaven is a reward in itself; a point on which all believers will undoubtedly agree. Yet, among the saved – those who are of the faith – it is evident that there are degrees of faith. There are those among the saved who are *more faithful* than others. The lives of some reflect a closer walk with God than do the lives of others. It stands to reason that those passages that speak to recompense speak to the idea of shades of rewards.

How will rewards be measured? They will be granted *according to deeds*. Works will serve as the objective scale upon which the faith of each redeemed person will be weighed. Those whose actions reflect a life of service and devotion to God – those who walk closest with God in this life – will receive the greater reward. This is a lesson that permeates the pages of Scripture, although the exact character of those rewards (blessings) remains undefined.

> Now the one who plants and the one who waters are one; but each will receive his own reward according to his own labor. (1 Corinthians 3: 8)

What is to be made of Paul's words to the Corinthians where he wrote about the testing of a person's works? How does the following text fit into the biblical lessons about God rendering to each one according to deeds?

> [12] Now if anyone builds on the foundation with gold, silver, precious stones, wood, hay, *or* straw, [13] each one's work will become evident; for the day will show it because it is *to be* revealed with fire, and the fire itself will test the quality of each one's work. [14] If anyone's work which he has built on it remains, he will receive a reward. [15] If anyone's work is burned up, he will suffer loss; but he himself will be saved, yet *only* so as through fire. (1 Corinthians 3: 12-15)

This is indeed a challenging text, and Bible scholars have offered varying opinions regarding Paul's meaning. What can be determined from Paul's words? First of all, this likely speaks to the review of the works of each believer on the Day of Judgment, though some have speculated that it deals more specifically with the works of Christian leaders. Others have suggested that Paul may be referring to wrongful doctrine sincerely taught and that those who did so will not be lost due to honest mistakes. Although a weak possibility, this seems to run contrary to Jesus' lesson about pseudo disciples (Matthew 7: 21-23).

Some think that Paul, in this passage, was dealing with the character, or identity of a person's works, considering the work of teachers, elders, etc., to be more substantive when compared to the work of the church janitor or the church secretary. Again, it is understandable how someone might draw that conclusion, but it does not seem to explain the idea that the person's work might be burned up, causing the person to suffer loss and still know salvation. A church janitor has a significant role in the church and can be as diligent and faithful a Christian as an elder or minister.

What follows here is not a claim to have 'the answer' to this difficult text, but a reasonable explanation seems to be that Paul was writing about the *quality* of the works of the believers (v. 13). Some will put greater effort into their work for the Lord than will others, and that work will have staying power. For example, the teacher who offers substantive instruction that sticks with his listeners will have undoubtedly put much effort into that teaching, searching Scripture diligently to assure that he is speaking God's truth. Teaching of a lesser quality, as a result of less effort, will have a smaller impact. While it may not measure up to the teaching that involved greater effort, it will not result in a loss of salvation simply because someone *could have done more* or *could have done better*.

It is doubtful that Jesus will weigh the works of individuals against the works of others, notwithstanding their position in the church. Those in leadership positions and teaching roles in the church will be held to a higher standard (cf. James 3: 10), but it seems likely that each person's work will stand on its own. Each one will be judged based on his/her individual effort to responsibly represent God and further the kingdom while on earth.

## Fingernails

It is not unusual to hear someone say that they are not concerned about special rewards…they simply want to make it to heaven, even if it means hanging on by their fingernails. The sentiment is understandable since no one is worthy of eternal life, and some make that kind of statement out of humility, realizing they will never deserve heaven.

Sadly, for others who make this kind of statement, it reflects a desire to do as little as possible in developing their relationship with God, but still know eternal life. It should go without saying that this is not what God expects from those who wish to spend eternity in heaven.

Walking with God is not about minimums. It is not a question of: *What can I get away with,* or *how little can I do, and still make it into heaven?* Rewards aside, the person who wishes to spend eternity with God should be working to develop the closest possible relationship with him. That is the person whose works will result in heavenly blessings. Rewards will come, not because someone can list an abundance of good works, but because that person put in the time and effort (work) to build his/her spiritual relationship with God – particularly when that effort is showered on other people (cf. Philippians 2: 3-4; 3 John 1: 5). That is what faithfulness is really all about.

# Summary

The biblical connection between faith and works is straightforward. It is a lesson taught forthrightly by Jesus, Peter, Paul, John, James, and the author of the book of Hebrews as well as other biblical writers. This lesson permeates the pages of both testaments. While attaining initial salvation is a matter of obedient faith, living a life of faith requires faithfulness, or active faith. Eternal life in heaven is reserved for the faithful. The Apostle John expressed Jesus' thoughts to the church in Smyrna, writing:

> Be faithful until death, and I will give you the crown of life. (Revelation 2: 10b)

Teaching faith without works may be attractive, since it seemingly lessens the burden for those who seek a place in heaven, but such teaching fails to withstand biblical scrutiny. Inactive faith is not the faith described in God's Word. James taught that "…faith also, if it has no works, is dead, *being* by itself" (James 2: 17). His point seems to be that the catchphrase *faith only* is a contradiction in terms. This may explain why Paul never used this expression.

A distinction must be drawn between good works and obedience. While no one can *earn* passage to heaven by performing good works, Scripture teaches that obedience to the terms of salvation proclaimed in the gospel message is the designated path to Jesus. In the covenant of grace, obedience to the precepts of the gospel is the *faith response* God expects to see from those who seek Jesus as their personal savior.

82

What many fail to recognize is that the precepts of the gospel message are personal for God. They represent not merely a set of conditions for attaining salvation, but they serve as the very means by which an individual honors God's decision to forgive the debt of mankind for sins committed by making the ultimate sacrifice – gracefully paying the debt himself.

Many believe Jesus' return is long overdue. In fact, some have inferred from Scripture that Paul thought the time of the Parousia was imminent even in the first century (cf. 1 Thessalonians 4: 15). Interestingly, people have been providing predictions of the time of the Parousia since late in the fourth century (perhaps even earlier) – often providing specific dates for the Parousia. So far, no prediction has withstood the test of time. Still, many continue to *prophesy*, giving dates that stretch into the middle of the twenty-first century.

The date for the Parousia is unknown, and it will remain unknown where humankind is concerned. It will come unexpectedly, as "…a thief in the night" (1 Thessalonians 5: 2). On that day, every person will receive just recompense for the life he/she has lived. For the lost, it will be a day of sorrowful reckoning. For the saved, it will be the beginning of unfathomable blessings.

# Bibliography

Did Martin Luther Really Want James Taken Out of… | Zondervan Academic.

Arnold, Clinton E., editor, *Zondervan Illustrated Bible Backgrounds Commentary, Volume 4: Hebrews to Revelation*, Zondervan, Grand Rapids, 2002.

Barnes, Albert, *Albert Barnes' Notes on the Whole Bible*, Matthew 19 - Albert Barnes' Notes on the Whole Bible - Bible Commentaries - StudyLight.org.

Carson, D. A., *The Expositor's Bible Commentary: Matthew*, Zondervan Publishing House, Grand Rapids, MI, 1995

Clark, Adam, *Clark's Commentaries, Volume VI, Romans – Revelation*, Abingdon-Cokesbury Press, New York/Nashville.

Coffman, James B., *James Burton Coffman Commentaries, Volume VI: Romans*, ACU Press, Houston, 1984.

Coffman, James, *James Burton Coffman Commentaries, Volume I: Matthew*, ACU Press, Abilene, TX, 1984.

Constable, Thomas, *Expository Notes of Dr. Thomas Constable*, Hebrews 8 - Expository Notes of Dr. Thomas Constable - Bible Commentaries - StudyLight.org

Constable, Thomas, *Expository Notes of Dr. Thomas Constable*, Hebrews 10 - Expository Notes of Dr. Thomas Constable - Bible Commentaries - StudyLight.org

Henry, Matthew, *Matthew Henry's Commentary on the Whole Bible: Complete and Unabridged*, Hendrickson Publishers, Inc., Peabody, MA

Lucado, Max, *In the Grip of Grace: Your Father Always Caught You. He Still Does*, Thomas Nelson, Nashville, Mexico City, Rio De Janeiro, 2014

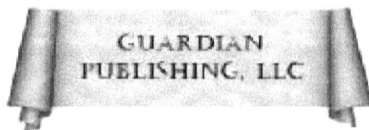

GUARDIAN
PUBLISHING, LLC

www.ingramcontent.com/pod-product-compliance
Lightning Source LLC
Chambersburg PA
CBHW031523040426
42445CB00009B/362